Problems of Philosophy and Psychology

Jay N. Eacker

Nelson-Hall
Chicago

Library of Congress Cataloging in Publication Data

Eacker, Jay N
    Problems of philosophy and psychology.

    Bibliography: p.
    Includes index.
    1. Psychology.   I. Title.
BF38.E13   150'.1   75-17548
ISBN 0-88229-202-1 (Hard cover)
ISBN 0-88229-489-X (Paper cover)

Contents

Acknowledgments

The author gratefully acknowledges permission to quote published material from the following authors, individuals, or publishers.

Bindra, D. *Motivation: A systematic reinterpretation.* New York. Copyright 1959 by The Ronald Press Company and reprinted by permission of the publisher.

Eacker, J.N. On more elementary philosophical problems of psychology. *JSAS Catalog of Selected Documents in Psychology,* 1974, 4, 35. (MS. No. 601). Copyright 1974 by the American Psychological Association and reprinted by permission of the publisher.

Eacker, J.N. On some elementary philosophical problems of psychology. *American Psychologist,* 1972, 27, 553-565. Copyright 1972 by the American Psychological Association and reprinted by permission of the publisher.

Hull, C.L. *Principles of behavior: An introduction to behavior theory.* New York. Copyright 1943 by Appleton-Century-Crofts and reprinted by permission of Dr. Richard H. Hull.

Hume, D. *An inquiry concerning human understanding.* Charles W. Hendel (Ed.). New York. Copyright 1955 by The Liberal Arts Press, Inc. and reprinted by permission of the publisher, The Bobbs-Merrill Company, Inc.

Hume, D. *A treatise of human nature.* L.A. Selby-Bigge (Ed.). London. Copyright 1888. Reprinted by permission of the publisher, The Clarendon Press.

Keller, F.S., & Schoenfeld, W.N. *Principles of behavior: A systematic text in*

Preface

What follows is an attempt to present, in a somewhat systematic way, certain problems of psychology that do not seem to be solvable with the methods of science. Nevertheless, each one of them is encountered again and again by psychologists and students of psychology as they become better acquainted with their discipline. In many cases, these problems simply are introduced as appropriate to the various subject matter areas of psychology, but they usually are not given the intensive treatment they require either then or at any other time. Even when they are given that kind of treatment, a consideration of how they are related to one another and to contemporary psychology may not be attempted. Perhaps the treatment of the problems in this book will help to correct such oversights.

The reader should not attempt to interpret many of the quoted passages too literally. They are taken from other contexts and, on that basis alone, may be misinterpreted in the present one. Aside from that, they have been cited for other reasons. The primary one is to acquaint all levels of students in psychology with what might be called the classical, or at least the most frequently referenced, literature on these problems from both philosophy and psychology; a glossary is included to facilitate the reading of it. Their inclusion provides the basis for considering these problems philosophical, but any effort to interpret them literally may lead away from the problem under discussion to others which, though related to it, must await their own examination.

This approach is taken and the warning issued because there may be many psychologists who have never read these passages and now perhaps cannot take the time to locate them in their primary sources because of other commitments. In addition, there may be many other students of psychology who have never read them and will not take the time that such scholarship requires. However, all students of psychology should be familiar with at least these portions of the original material because without that minimum familiarity they may fail to see just where these problems belong in the history of the discipline; this method may be one of the least painful means of accomplishing that end.

There are many unnamed acquaintances, colleagues, mentors, and students who have influenced this project. There are many others who are namable but who might prefer to remain anonymous. Nevertheless, some of them must be mentioned if only to repay in some small way their various contributions to these efforts. The following have contributed, some more than others, to the present work although none is responsible for the final product. They are: Edward C. Moore, F. Dudley Klopfer, Walter H. Brattain, Henry Margenau, Marianne Peterson, G.W. Brown, and J.J. Maier.

In addition, J. Michael Rona deserves special mention for an undergraduate honors thesis on the fact-value problem in psychology that aided immeasurably in the articulation of views on that problem. The work was completed in large part on a sabbatical leave and was funded over several summers by aid-to-faculty scholarship grants from Whitman College. Finally, but not least, some reference must be made to the inestimable contribution of some special girls, Anna, Anne, and Jane, who may not have realized just how important their help was.

1

Introduction

Some time ago, the philosopher Bertrand Russell wrote a small book entitled *The Problems of Philosophy* (1912). In it, he discussed such things as appearance and reality, the existence of matter, idealism, induction, and knowledge. A relatively short time ago, the psychologist Sigmund Koch (1956, p. 83) had occasion to remark, "It is barely possible that the mark of maturity of a science *is the maturity to face its own problems"*; the science to which he referred was, of course, psychology.

The problems of philosophy are not necessarily the problems of psychology, although it would be foolish to deny that some of them might be. That is, some of the problems referred to by Koch may be the same as those discussed by Russell. Perhaps psychology has matured to the point at which an examination of at least some of its philosophical problems is in order; what follows is a first attempt at that task.

In general, there seem to be two major classes of problems with which psychology is concerned. There are those that apparently can be solved with the methods of science and those that cannot. The first are scientific whereas the second are philosophical, but these two classes are not necessarily mutually exclusive; scientific problems may involve philosophical ones and vice versa.

The terms in which a scientific problem statement or question is posed apparently can be operationally defined in such a way that an answer to it, at least in principle, can be obtained with the empirical methods of science or observation. An example of this kind of problem is illustrated by the question "Is novelty reinforcing?" In that form the question cannot be answered observationally because the terms used to express it are not sufficiently clear. However, they can be clarified by defining a novel stimulus as one that a given organism has never encountered before or at least not within the recent past (cf. Berlyne, 1960, pp. 19-20). Similarly, a reinforcing stimulus can be defined as one that, when contingent upon a response, increases the rate of responses that produce it in the case of positive reinforcement, or that remove it in the case of negative reinforcement (cf. Skinner, 1953, p. 73). The question then becomes "Does a stimulus that has never been encountered before increase the rate of responses that produce, or remove, it?"

However, even in that form the question is not sufficiently clear because the particular stimulus to be considered novel has not yet been specified, and the same is true for the type of response. It is only after they have that a scientific question is reduced to a form in which observations can be performed to answer it. Thus, the question finally submitted for observational test might be "Does an illumination change of four foot-candles (which the subject has never encountered before) increase the rate of bar presses that produce it?" Or, it might be "Does an auditory change of one decibel (which the subject has not encountered before) increase the rate of bar contacts that produce it?"

At this point it is of some importance to note that in the process of operational reduction, the question has changed from an "is" form to a "does" form. The "is" form of the question is existential; it asks whether something exists, and the methods of science apparently cannot be used to answer existential questions. The "does" form of the question is functional; it asks what is related to what, and these descriptive kinds of questions appear to be the ones that the methods of science were especially developed to answer. These considerations illustrate how philosophical problems may be inseparable from scientific ones.

In addition, of course, the language of the question has been altered from that of "novelty" to that of "stimulus change," and there is lingering controversy over whether that kind of translation is permissible; it is controversy of that sort that leads to further experimentation in science. Nevertheless, it is by some such process as has been described that scientific problems are operationally defined. The terms of the problem are reduced to some form of measurement, and "when description gives way to measurement, calculation replaces debate" (Stevens, 1951, p. 1).

The same apparently cannot be said of philosophical problems; they are still matters for debate. There

3

does not yet appear to be any way in which questions of this type can be reduced to measurement operations, although they may at some time in the future. For example, a question in the form "What is the nature of reality?" is a statement of the philosophical problem of metaphysics or ontology. There does not now appear to be any way in which critical terms in the question such as "nature" and "reality" can be reduced to measurement, and it is not entirely clear how the question might be rephrased to make it more susceptible to operational analysis.

Another example of a question of this type is "Why is a reinforcer reinforcing?" If the question as posed requires an answer in some ultimate sense such as the basic nature of reinforcement, it is like the previous question about reality and is at present unanswerable with the methods of science. On the other hand, there are some occasions when reinforcers are reinforcing and some when they are not; food may not reinforce a food satiated animal. Hence, the question might be rephrased "What makes a reinforcer reinforcing?" and if that is considered equivalent to "Why is a reinforcer reinforcing?" then the answer to it is some kind of deprivation operation. This second situation illustrates how scientific problems may be inseparable from philosophic ones.

Nevertheless, there are some problems that cannot be rephrased in that way, and even if they could, there are those who would reject the translation. There are many people who would not accept the assertion that the question "Why is a reinforcer reinforcing?" is equivalent to the question "What makes a reinforcer reinforcing?" For that matter, there are those who might not accept deprivation operations as an answer to the question "What makes a reinforcer reinforcing?" but who would require, instead, one based on a theory of evolution or, perhaps, creation. It is this second category of problems that provides the subject matter for the present work.

The scientific problems of psychology receive, as they should, the major proportion of consideration in the journals, monographs, and textbooks of psychology today; the philosophical problems are sometimes considered but are most frequently ignored. However, it may be that the philosophical problems give rise to at least some of the scientific ones, and so a systematic treatment of some of the former may help to clarify some of the latter. In addition, philosophical problems may obtrude into scientific ones at points where they are least expected, and they may require some minimum consideration before the scientist can get on with the task of solving the scientific problems with which he is confronted. For example, there are very few psychologists concerned with the scientific problems of learning who would question whether learning phenomena exist. However, it could happen that they do not exist but are simply constructed, and consideration of that possibility might lead to some new ways of formulating some old scientific problems of learning.

This situation was illustrated in part by Edna Heidbreder (1933, p. 326) when she remarked:

> It is true that some of the most brilliant achievements of science have been accomplished by the method of combat—by championing a hypothesis against every kind of opposition until it is proved right or wrong, or partly right and partly wrong. But this is only one of the ways in which

science wins its successes. Sometimes it gains its victories through the workers who are so interested in the particular problems of a particular class of facts that they deliberately postpone or ignore, for the time, the consideration of the more remote and far-reaching implications of those problems.

Perhaps now is an appropriate time to consider some of "the more remote and far-reaching implications of those problems."

Historically, psychology has moved from an almost exclusive preoccupation with philosophical problems to the point at which it nearly denies them. This situation probably developed normally in the course of the evolution of psychology away from philosophy toward natural science. However, many if not all of the philosophical problems still persist in at least some form within psychology today, and so a close consideration of them is in order if only for purposes of clarification.

A systematic treatment of the philosophical problems of psychology is not only of some importance for the discipline as a whole; it is also of some significance for individual psychologists, students of psychology, and informed laymen who develop an interest in psychology. As psychology becomes less and less philosophical, fewer and fewer psychologists are exposed to its persisting philosophical problems. This state of affairs may be detrimental to the evolution of the science and especially with respect to the way in which psychologists conceptualize what they are doing. They may come to the view that the problems of psychology are not the problems of philosophy and that the two disciplines, if philosophy can be called a discipline, have little in common. No conclusion could be more in error since, as already suggested, many of the problems of psychology originated, and may still originate, in philosophy and since psychology is of interest to philosophy if only by way of its philosophy of science.

In addition, there are many psychologists who have never had occasion at least to doubt that they discover, for example, the phenomena and laws of learning or motivation in the behavioral laboratory, that the terms *learning* and *motivation* may not refer to unique classes of events. There may be other psychologists who have never considered the possibility that the denial, or ignorance, of metaphysics is metaphysical. This possibility is illustrated in another remark by Heidbreder (1933, p. 326) when she stated:

> More often than not, the logically opposed alternatives that have confronted each other through long ages, make their appeal to human interest either directly or indirectly through the metaphysical implications which surround them. But whatever progress science has made has come through deliberately turning its attention away from the problems of the ultimate. For this reason psychology in particular, all the more because it is a young science and was very recently a part of philosophy, is on its guard against metaphysics; so much so, in fact, that a system of psychology may adopt, either deliberately or unintentionally, a metaphysics to justify its dismissal of the problems it considers metaphysical.

Still other psychologists may never have entertained the possibility that science may not, in fact, be what the philosophers of science have said it is; that a new science, such as psychology, based on the old conception of science is obsolete before it even has been fully articulated; that some sciences may differ so radically from the others that the unification of science is simply not a possibility; that psychology may not be a science of behavior so much as it is a science of observed events, which may also be true of the other sciences; and, that physical concepts such as force are perhaps inappropriate in explanations of behavior or observed events of the type examined by psychologists.

Similarly, students of psychology and those who develop more than a casual interest in psychology frequently begin their study on the assumption that the philosophical problems of psychology are what psychology is all about; they may even go so far as to suppose that it is those problems that define psychology. In addition, each new generation of college students in general, and psychology students in particular, seem to require that the philosophical problems at least be examined and perhaps resolved anew. Hence, the philosophical problems of psychology are of enduring interest to its students no matter what their level of sophistication; it is especially for them that this discussion is intended.

In a fairly recent work, Klein (1970, p. 220) remarked:

In preparation for his tribute to the memory of William James, Gordon Allport evidently reread the *Principles* and was struck by certain contradictions in what James had to say in the course of his treatment of given topics. Allport's article deals with these contradictions as products of some of psychology's pivotal problems. They have to do with cardinal issues that lie embedded in psychology's philosophic past and continue to have relevance for psychology's scientific present. As a consequence they may be thought of as guidelines for a perplexed historian trying to find his way through the complex maze of events having either a direct or indirect bearing on the long history of psychology. As persistent problems of psychology they run through the warp and woof of the pattern of its history; hence their usefulness as criteria to aid in discriminating the historically relevant from the irrelevant. They are broad enough in their implications to encompass the major criteria governing the historian's selective perception. In his article Allport refers to them as "the persistent riddles of psychology" likely to puzzle every psychologist in the course of his professional endeavors.

These "riddles" deal with complex questions for which there are no assured answers. Seen from one viewpoint one set of answers seems plausible, but from a different and equally tenable viewpoint another set of answers may seem equally plausible. The result is apparent contradiction or inconsistency, especially if one discusses them in terms of such divergent viewpoints. This lack of agreement makes them paradoxical and productive of thought-provoking reflection. At least William James wrestled with each of them in earnest if ambivalent fashion. In Allport's wording, they may be called "the productive paradoxes of William James."

According to Allport (1943), there were six of them. They were: the psychophysical riddle or the mind-body problem; the riddle of positivism; the riddle of the self; the riddle of free will or freedom; the riddle of association; and, the riddle of individuality.

In still more recent works, Lundin (1972) listed what he referred to as basic issues of psychology. His list included: mind versus body; subjectivism versus objectivism; quantification versus qualification; reductionism versus nonreductionism; molar versus molecular; determinism versus teleology; utility versus purity; nativism versus empiricism; and reward versus nonreward. Similarly, Wertheimer (1972) enumerated some dozen or so substantive and methodological, but fundamental, issues in psychology including, among others, mind versus body, subjectivity versus objectivity, nature versus nurture, and theory versus data; it may not be entirely out of order to wonder whether these dichotomies are functions of the problems or the logic used to examine them. Nevertheless, it is clear that there is no dearth of issues that could be examined although they all might not be philosophical problems of psychology, and the list constructed by one psychologist might not include all of those listed by another.

For present purposes, the number is restricted to thirteen philosophical problems in the sense proposed earlier. It includes some of those mentioned in every list, some that were included on only one or two, and some not found on any of the above lists. The thirteen problems are: the mind-body problem, metaphysics, reification, explanation, causality, theory, laws and principles, anthropomorphism, purpose, freedom, knowledge, induction, and the fact-value problem. They are by no means either mutually exclusive or exhaustive, and they are discussed in the order in which they were listed because they seem logically to follow one from the other in that order. After they have been presented and examined, an attempt will be made to indicate how they are relevant to contemporary psychology. The task is undertaken in the hope that psychologists, and other students of psychology, will find that it facilitates their own examination and resolution of these same problems.

2

The Mind-Body Problem

I n his book *Body and Mind* (ca. 1911), William McDougall (1928, p. vii) attempted to provide students of psychology and philosophy with "a critical survey of modern opinion and discussion upon the psycho-physical problem, the problem of the relation between body and mind." A few sentences later, he observed that "among the great questions debated by philosophers in every age the psycho-physical problem occupies a special position, in that it is one in which no thoughtful person can fail to be interested. . . ." The basis for that interest may have changed somewhat over the years, especially among psychologists, but there is no doubt that it still remains a problem for debate; the methods of science are not likely to solve it, as will be evident toward the close of this discussion.

According to McDougall (1928, p. 20):

> Plato purified the conception of the soul of the last remnants of the dualistic materialism of primitive Animism, which still lingered in the Orphic doctrine, and, insisting upon the fundamental difference of nature between soul and body, clearly formulated for the first time the theory of psycho-physical dualism with reciprocal action between soul and body.

A somewhat more modern version of the problem was formulated by René Descartes (ca. 1641), and it has since been referred to as the Cartesian Myth (cf. Ryle, 1949, pp. 11-24). In his sixth *Meditation,* and elsewhere, Descartes (in Haldane and Ross, trans., 1931, p. 90) deduced that what distinguished man from the other animals was that the human one consisted of two quite unlike substances. One of them was a substance with the major, if not sole, attribute of thought. The other was a substance with, among other attributes, those of length, breadth, and width; it was an extended substance. The first was an unextended, but thinking, substance and the second was an extended, but unthinking, substance. The problem was how two such unlike substances could possibly influence one another.

McDougall's was, for its time, perhaps one of the most scholarly and exhaustive treatments of this problem in the history of psychology. In it, he traced the problem from primitive animism or, in his own words, anthropomorphism, which indicates once more how intimately the philosophical problems of psychology are related. In the process, he mentioned some twenty or more solutions to the problem, although not all of them were mutually exclusive and some were not necessarily intended as solutions.

Those mentioned were: interactionism, occasionalism, psychophysical parallelism, the double aspect hypothesis, epiphenomenalism, the identity hypothesis, materialism, idealism, and some less well known ones that appear to be simply variations on this first group. The remaining ones were: animistic dualism, parallelistic animism, phenomenalistic parallelism, hylozoism, psychoneural concomitance, sensationalism, psychical monism, subjective idealism, phenomenalism, animism, vitalism, transformation theory, transmission theory, and soul theory. According to Klein (1970, p. 230), a complete listing of the various solutions that have occurred over the years might number close to thirty.

Most authors usually examine some seven or eight of what might be called the major solutions in their discussions of the problem and sometimes classify them according to whether they represent a monistic or a dualistic view of man; that is, whether man is viewed as composed of one substance or two. For example, Muenzinger (1942, pp. 413-14) referred to interactionism, psychophysical parallelism, epiphenomenalism, the double aspect theory, the double language hypothesis, materialistic monism, and idealistic monism among the major solutions to the problem. Similarly, Marx and Hillix (1963, p. 27) listed interactionism, psychophysical parallelism, and occasionalism as dualisms; materialism, subjective idealism, and phenomenalism as monisms; and the double aspect hypothesis and epiphenomenalism as compromises. The more frequently examined solutions in these and other sources appear to be interactionism, psychophysical parallelism, occasionalism, epiphenomenalism, the double aspect hypothesis, idealism, materialism, and the identity hypothesis.

Interactionism is a dualistic solution to the problem. It is the view that the two substances of which man is composed, mind and body, interact with one another even though they are basically different in nature. This solution is most often attributed to Descartes, who developed it further with the suggestion that the interaction occurred through the mediation of the pineal body in the brain. That is, when mind influenced body, the animal spirits in the nerves and brain were inclined in one direction by the pineal gland, and when body influenced mind, the gland inclined the spirits in the other direction (cf. Boring, 1957a, p. 164).

Psychophysical parallelism is also a dualistic solution to the problem. According to this view, man is composed of two substances, mind and body, but they do not interact; they parallel one another. The functions of the mind essentially parallel the functions of the body, but they remain independent of one another. Each follows its own laws, exhibits perfect agreement with the other, and both give the appearance of interaction but they do not, in fact, do so. Gottfried Wilhelm Leibnitz (ca. 1714) is most often credited with this view; apparently, it is a logical corollary of his monadology as well as his doctrine of pre-established harmony (cf. Watson, 1971, p. 168).

Occasionalism is another dualistic solution to the mind-body problem and is frequently attributed to Arnold Geulincx (ca. 1655); according to Klein (1970, p. 352), it antedated parallelism. Occasionalism is the view that a deity intervened on those occasions when mind influenced, or appeared to influence, body. Mind and body were different substances as in the Cartesian formulation of the problem; their interaction, or apparent interaction, was occasioned by the intervention of a divine being.

A fourth dualistic solution, since it requires at least a phenomenon and a substance rather than two substances, is epiphenomenalism. This solution to the problem asserts that the phenomena of mind simply accompany the actions of the body but are not an essential part of them, much like the foam on a glass of beer accompanies, but is not crucial for, the loss of carbonation; with respect to the loss of carbonation, the foam is an epiphenomenon. Thomas Henry Huxley (ca. 1863) was apparently one of the major proponents of this view (cf. Capretta, 1967, pp. 18-20).

The double aspect hypothesis is a monistic solution to the problem in the sense that there is only one substance considered from two different perspectives or aspects. Body and mind are but two aspects of a single underlying reality. What appears as mind from one perspective appears as body from the other. Benedict Baruch Spinoza (ca. 1677) seems to have arrived at this position by way of his theological speculations; according to Watson (1971, p. 166), it is a monistic parallelism.

A second monistic solution to the mind-body problem is idealism, subjective idealism, phenomenalism, sensationalism, sensationism, or psychical monism. Since it affirms only the existence of ideas, subjective phenomena, sensations, sense experience, or mental events, it eliminates the problem. If there is only mind, the question of how mind influences body does not arise. According to this view, there are only ideas or mental events; mind is the basic reality. All that can be known are ideas, mental events, or sense experience. Bodies, matter, or objects, if they exist at all, cannot be known to exist except by means of sense experience. They cannot be known to exist independently of sense experience; to be is to be perceived. Things exist only as, or to the extent that, they are perceived or sensed (cf. Klein, 1970, p. 232). Hence, bodies are in minds; they do not influence minds. This solution, if it can be called that, is essentially a metaphysical, or ontological, position that was offered not so much to solve the mind-body problem as to deal with other issues, especially the problem of knowledge; in the process, it did away with the mind-body problem. George Berkeley (ca. 1709) is usually considered the author of this solution although it was basically an extension of work begun by John Locke (ca. 1690) and was developed further by David Hume (ca. 1738), as will be seen in the discussion of the problem of metaphysics.

Another essentially ontological position that does away with the problem is materialism, materialistic monism, or realism; there are some similarities between it and positivism except that positivism attempted to avoid metaphysical speculations. In psychology, this solution is most often associated with John Broadus Watson (ca. 1913), although Thomas Hobbes (ca. 1650) may also receive some mention in connection with it (cf. Muenzinger, 1942, p. 414; Watson, 1971, p. 181). According to this monistic solution to the problem, all that exists is body or matter. Mind either does not exist or, if it does, is not remarkably different from body or physiological processes. Proponents of this view may not so much deny the existence of mind as they ignore it or at least consider the assumption of consciousness, mind, or mental events as somewhat arbitrary. Nevertheless, regardless of whether or not mental events exist, this solution also eliminates the problem, since what is of importance is the physical body and, more especially, what it does.

The identity hypothesis may or may not be a major solution to the mind-body problem because it has so much in common with the double aspect theory (cf. Klein, 1970, p. 233) and idealism. According to McDougall (1928, p. 133), it takes two forms, which he referred to as phenomenalistic parallelism, and psychical monism. The first form was attributed to both Spinoza and Immanuel Kant and "implies the metaphysical doctrine known as realistic Monism. It asserts that reality or real being, of which mind and body are appearances only, is not immediately given to or known by us."

The second "form of the identity-hypothesis implies a metaphysical doctrine which is usually designated idealistic Monism, but is better described as realistic or objective psychical Monism"; hence, it is about the same as the solution identified earlier as idealism and attributed to Berkeley. However, according to Boring (1957a, p. 667), the identity theory "is like the double-aspect theory except that it overlooks the difference in methods of observation and concentrates on the underlying reality (construct) as what is observed. It makes introspection into a method for observing the functioning of the brain." Despite these assurances, the identity hypothesis may eventually be eliminated as one of the major solutions to the mind-body problem because it is so similar to the double aspect theory and idealism.

A solution that may take its place, although it is

now seldom discussed as a major solution to the mind-body problem, is the doctrine of isomorphism. According to Boring (1957a, p. 615):

> There is nothing inherent in Gestalt psychology that requires any particular mind-body theory; yet the three principal Gestalt psychologists have all supported isomorphism—the theory that the perceptual field corresponds with the underlying excitatory brain field in its relations of order, although not necessarily in exact form. The correspondence is topological but not topographical. Adjacent spots in one system match adjacent spots in the other, but a shape in one may be greatly distorted in the other.

This solution apparently was first formulated by Max Wertheimer (ca. 1912) but was supported in the writings of Kurt Koffka and Wolfgang Kohler. It seems to be a dualistic solution since it requires, on the one hand, sense experience and, on the other, neural excitation.

What is perhaps a variation on the materialism, or materialistic monism, of Watson has appeared more recently in the work of B.F. Skinner (1953, pp. 257-82), although he by no means offered it as a solution to the mind-body problem. He stated that the chief difference between what goes on inside man, as well as other organisms perhaps, and what goes on outside him is simply that what goes on inside is less public. Nevertheless, what goes on inside might be thought of as the same as what goes on outside, namely, behavior. The behavior of seeing is simply what the eye does, the behavior of hearing is what the ear does, and so on through all the distinguishable receptor systems. These behaviors differ from those of, for example, walking or bar pressing only to the extent that the latter can be observed while the former cannot; the former are covert whereas the latter are overt. Consequently, psychologists should not be surprised to find that principles of behavior based on observations of overt behavior are entirely consistent with, and can be extrapolated to explain, covert behavior. This statement appears to express the problem with which Descartes dealt in the first place, except that he attempted to proceed from what went on inside to what went on outside. Skinner would reverse the process; he would use the outer man to explain the inner one rather than the other way around as appears to have been the case with Descartes, who may have been too much in awe of the inner man.

None of the solutions proposed has yet been accepted as definitive. In fact, it appears rather doubtful that any ever will be. For example, Muenzinger (1942, pp. 414-15) has observed:

In psychology the mind-body problem requires a radical reformulation. In a science we can deal only with the interrelations of observed events. Any theory, assumption, or problem must refer to concrete relationships. Therefore the only way in which we can formulate the mind-body problem in psychology is in terms of physiological processes and behavior as the two sets of observed events to be correlated. When this is done the seven philosophical solutions of the problem are irrelevant to what the psychologist does. No matter which one of these solutions the psychologist may favor, all he can study is the interrelation between the body and behavior. The psychological formulation of the problem is the only one that can be dealt with concretely and experimentally. Moreover, it does not demand a solution but a continuous experimental attack.

There are those psychologists who might object that the task of psychology is not to determine the relations between body and behavior but, rather, the relations between behavior and the variables of which it is a function. Nevertheless, they probably would accept his conclusion that the solutions are irrelevant to what psychologists do, at least in the experimental areas.

For example, John Broadus Watson (1913, p. 166), who is often referred to as the father of behaviorism, expressed the view that

> *behaviorism* is the only consistent and logical functionalism. In it one avoids both the Scylla of parallelism and the Charybdis of interaction. Those time-honored relics of philosophical speculation need trouble the student of behavior as little as they trouble the student of physics. The consideration of the mind-body problem affects neither the type of problem selected nor the formulation of the solution of that problem. I can state my position here no better than by saying that I should like to bring my students up in the same ignorance of such hypotheses as one finds among the students of other branches of science.

On the other hand, Boring (1957a, p. 668) concluded from his analysis of the problem that:

These theories have become less important with the advance of operational thinking. It is now taken for granted that the same generality is found by many different observational techniques which supplement and confirm each other. Even when twentieth-century psychologists refuse to accept physicalism, still they are apt to find dualism less important than did their teachers and their teachers' teachers.

More explicit development of this position is contained in the statements of recent authors who have found it appropriate to comment on the problem. For example, Turner (1971, p. 169) observed:

Doubtless a major difficulty in writing about consciousness and awareness, even at this late date, is that no one is able precisely to define what it is that either he would affirm or he would deny. For scientists, at least, it would appear that the conundrums of mind-body dualism are passé, if for no other reason than empirical tests of hypotheses are found wanting. . . .

Similarly, Klein (1970, p. 229) contradicted Watson with the observation that:

there is no way of settling the problem even today. As yet the rival psychophysical views do not lend themselves to experimental investigation. They are not amenable to the kind of formulation that results in testable hypotheses. Dealing as they do with the ultimate nature of existence, they belong to the realm of metaphysics rather than to that of empirical science. This is not to say that they are now devoid of influence on the outlook of the scientific psychologist. In terms of an implicit faith or temperamental bias, he is likely to find himself having preferences with respect to the metaphysical options. Those whom James called tough-minded are apt to have different preferences from the tender-minded. Such preferences tend to color one's psychologizing. Without being a professional metaphysician, every psychologist is influenced by metaphysical considerations—by his hunches or beliefs regarding the ultimate nature of the universe. This is true even of those who pride themselves on their lack of interest in metaphysics.

It is to be hoped that contemporary psychologists no longer psychologize in the manner exemplified by James. Hopes aside, these remarks indicate that, while the problem may not lead to experiments designed to solve it, it may nevertheless have some influence on experiments designed to solve other kinds of problems, contrary to Watson's pronouncements. Such considerations lead the discussion into the problem of metaphysics, but they also support the selection of the mind-body problem as a philosophical problem of psychology; there does not appear to be any way to solve it with an empirical test.

3

The Problem of
Metaphysics

T his problem received considerable mention in
    the introduction and in the discussion of the
previous problem, and so now may be an appropriate
time to examine it. For some time, the term metaphysics "has tended to designate two large branches of
thought: ontology and epistemology . . ." (Margenau,
1950, pp. 80-81). Ontology has to do with the philosophical question of what there is, whereas epistemology has to do with the question of how we know what
there is; consequently, discussions of one will almost
inevitably shade into discussions of the other. Nevertheless, the present discussion attempts to deal only
with the question of what there is, or ontology, but
equates ontology with metaphysics since the latter term
probably is more familiar to psychologists, students of
psychology, and informed laymen who develop an

interest in psychology; the problem of knowledge, or epistemology, will be dealt with later.

Philosophical speculations about what there is can be said to vary all the way from the single substance, or "one-stuff," cosmogonies of the pre-Socratic philosophers to the sophisticated cosmologies of the post-Kantian pragmatists, although there are those who would draw finer distinctions between ontology, cosmogony, and cosmology. Despite these considerations, there are at least two ontological, or metaphysical, positions that are possible for science in general and behavioral science in particular. They are: realism and phenomenalism; the problem is which one to adopt.

That adoption of metaphysical, or ontological, positions occurs among contemporary psychologists is amply demonstrated in remarks by recent authors and especially historians of psychology. For example, Klein (1970, p. 839) stated:

> It may not be too much of a digression to note that psychologists of the modern era do not always succeed in avoiding metaphysical commitments despite their efforts to do so. Although they rarely give direct consideration to questions of monism, parallelism, and similar obviously metaphysical issues, they sometimes give them indirect consideration by allusions to concepts like *mentalism* and *physicalism*. Those who define psychology as the science of behavior take a dim view of "mentalistic" reports of conscious contents and of phenomenological descriptions of experience. In calling such reports and descriptions "mentalistic," they are objecting to the animistic connotation they attribute to the doctrine of mentalism. In general,

because of this connotation they would object to having psychology defined as the science of mind or consciousness. As they see it, words like "mind" or "consciousness" may be subtle synonyms for the word "soul" and as such may interfere with efforts to keep psychology within the realm of science. . . .

His remarks were uttered in relation to some issues encountered by Wilhelm Wundt (ca. 1879), who is frequently referred to as the father of experimental psychology. However, they apply more generally to all psychologists; the avoidance of metaphysical commitments may presuppose a metaphysical commitment at least according to a logical analysis. Hence, rather than avoid such commitments, it may be simpler to acknowledge them and then attempt to make them more explicit. "The logical positivists learned long ago that anti-metaphysics, and all the protestations, lead nowhere if not to metaphysics" (Turner, 1968, p. vii).

The two metaphysical positions that may be taken in science are frequently presented as materialism and idealism or realism and idealism, but the terms realism and phenomenalism have been chosen to avoid some possible ambiguities related to pairing the words realism and idealism. That is, it is fairly common practice to regard an idealist as one who acts according to some preconception of how things ought to be rather than according to how things are, whereas one who acts according to how things are, granted that it is possible to know how things are, is commonly referred to as a realist. When used in these ways, both terms are relevant more to right conduct, or ethics, than they are to metaphysics.

The first metaphysical position, realism, is familiar to everyone; most people are uncritical, or naive, realists. They find it absurd to question the view that a real, objective world exists, with real objects and phenomena in it, and that it would continue to exist whether there were anyone around to observe it or not; that is, it exists independently of any observer. Furthermore, it is this world that is discovered through the application of the methodology of science.

On first impression, we all seem to be realists. When the child sees the internal mechanism of the clock with its springs and gears, he is satisfied that there is no mystery to the rotating hands. If the cosmologist pursues the retreating galaxies for one more clue to an evolving universe, he is likely to think of himself as learning what the universe is, or was, really like. And if the psychologist sees perceptual invariance emerging from neural integration over equivalence classes of input, he is likely to put aside his heuristic devices and proclaim the truth as to the nature of perception. . . . [Turner, 1967, p. 170]

This view probably originated in the common sense of early man but is somewhat difficult to trace in the history of philosophy. Thales (ca. 600 B.C.), who is often referred to as the father of Western philosophy, was probably a realist in metaphysics since he argued for the emergence of all things from water. That is, water and all things in the world, which develop out of it, were apparently real. Plato can be described as a realist since he held that ideas are independent of and more real than sensible objects. In that sense, he can be called a realistic idealist since ideas were real and existent; hence, realism and idealism are not necessarily opposed metaphysical positions. Regardless of its origins, realism will probably persist since it makes such good sense to common sense and is perhaps simpler than phenomenalism.

This second metaphysical position, phenomenalism, is not so familiar to everyone, and there is at least one remaining ambiguity related to the use of that term that must be discussed before the position can be presented. Spence (1956, p. 7) equated phenomenalism with phenomenology in psychology and then went on to discuss the latter as the former. However, rather than a metaphysical position, phenomenology in psychology appears to be more a point of view adopted at an early stage in the historical development of psychology that was related primarily to methodology. That is, it accepted the verbal reports of subjective experience by untrained observers as valid subject matter for psychological investigation as opposed to introspectionism, which would accept only the verbal reports of those trained in the special method of introspection; this distinction was perhaps first made by the Gestalt psychologist Wolfgang Kohler (1938, p. 105). A variation on this view continues within psychology at the present time (cf. Wann, 1964), but it probably differs somewhat from phenomenology in contemporary philosophy.

By contrast, the metaphysical position here referred to as phenomenalism is that what exists is whatever it is that occurs when the senses experience, that is, sense experience. The phenomenalist does not assert that a real, objective world exists with real objects and phenomena in it. Rather, he simply affirms that what he knows, perhaps directly, is sense experience, although he may not be able to answer when asked to say what it is; the same might be true of the realist if he were asked to say what the real world is. Consequently, the world is constructed by the phenomenalist out of his own sense experience as well as that of others; the world, or his conception of it, develops out of the application of the methodology of science.

This view did not necessarily originate but was certainly elaborated in the writings of George Berkeley, Bishop of Cloyne (ca. 1710), although in his case it frequently is referred to, perhaps erroneously, as subjective idealism. The position adopted by Berkeley was further developed by David Hume (ca. 1738), and it is this development that is commonly regarded as phenomenalism. It should be stressed, however, that it is most often thought of as an epistemology (cf. Turner, 1967, p. 53); nevertheless, when it affirms sense experience, or the existence of same, it can be considered as an ontology.

Perhaps Hume's conception is best illustrated in his discussion of modes and substances, and particularly substance. He stated that the ideas of both are essentially collections of simple ideas united by imagination.

But the difference betwixt these ideas consists in this, that the particular qualities, which form a substance, are commonly refer'd to an unknown *something,* in which they are supposed to inhere; or granting this fiction should not take place, are at least supposed to be closely and inseparably connected by the relations of contiguity and causation. [Hume, 1888, p. 16]

30

The "unknown something" in which qualities were "supposed to inhere" is the object of the idea or the real world for the realist, but it is a fiction for Hume. What is real, or at least existent, are the impressions of "sensation, passions, and emotions" of which ideas are the faint images "in thinking and reasoning" (Hume, 1888, p. 1).

A more recent statement of phenomenalism for psychologists asserted:

> Phenomenalism follows the empiricist tradition, i.e., all knowledge of the external world is made contingent upon perception; but it is even more explicit in its reducing knowledge of material objects to sense contents, and to sense contents alone. Thus, for phenomenalism, all ontological statements are reducible to statements whose meanings are assignable only in terms of empirical constituents. [Turner, 1967, p. 53]

What the phenomenalist claims is sensation, sense experience, or sense contents. He does not, or cannot, say what they are or what they are of. They simply occur, and out of them, as a scientist, he constructs his view of physical reality (cf. Margenau, 1950).

It is of some interest to compare these two positions with respect to the activities of scientists, behavioral or otherwise, who might hold either of them in apparent opposition. As scientists, they would both be empiricists, that is, they would both subscribe to the observational basis of knowledge in science. Hence, both would employ the experimental methodology of science; their laboratory behaviors probably would not differ. The chief difference between them would seem to be in what they did with their observations. The realist would tend to "put aside his heuristic devices and proclaim the truth as to the nature" of the universe. He would argue from his observations, that is, his sense experience, to a realm of objects or behavioral events, which, if known, could be known at all only through sense experience; he would "go beyond his data." By contrast, the phenomenalist would tend to stop at the point of observation and perhaps emphasize the fact that his knowledge claims, and those of others, were limited to, or by, sense experience.

Since realism has been the traditional and predominant metaphysical position in science, and since phenomenalism appears equally defensible though perhaps less appealing to common sense, the metaphysical problem for psychologists is which one of them to adopt. Realism has been tried; phenomenalism might well lead to greater theoretical and experimental insights than have so far been obtained, especially in those sciences concerned with what are called observed events, or behavior, as opposed to observed objects.

4

The Problem of
Reification

Reification is a philosophical problem of psychology regardless of which metaphysical position might be adopted, but it may especially be one for realism; at least one author has referred to it as a "metaphysical sin" (cf. Kaplan, 1964, p. 61). As Carnap (1956, p. 22) understood it, "a hypostatization or substantialization or reification consists in mistaking as things entities which are not things"; Reichenbach (1951, p. 12) used the phrase "substantialization of abstracta" to describe the case in which "an abstract noun, like 'reason,' is treated as though it refers to some thing-like entity." For Hull (1943, p. 28), "to reify a function is to give it a name and presently to consider that the name represents a thing, and finally to believe that the thing so named somehow explains the performance of the function. . . ." As with the problem of anthropomorphism to be examined later, reification refers to a particular practice that has been engaged in from time to time by psychologists and apparently one that is to be avoided.

An example of the practice in modern psychology has been described by B.F. Skinner (1953, p. 202), although he did not refer to it as reification.

> Trait-names usually begin as adjectives— "intelligent," "aggressive," "disorganized," "angry," "introverted," "nervous," and so on—but the almost inevitable linguistic result is that adjectives give birth to nouns. The things to which these nouns refer are then taken to be the active causes of the aspects. We begin with "intelligent behavior," pass first to "behavior which *shows* intelligence," and then to "behavior which *is the effect of* intelligence." Similarly, we begin by observing a preoccupation with a mirror which recalls the legend of Narcissus; we invent the adjective "narcissistic," and then the noun "narcissism"; and finally we assert that the thing presumably referred to by the noun is the cause of the behavior with which we began. . . .

Instances of efforts to curb the practice of reification in psychology are not difficult to find. For example, Peters (1963, pp. 437-38) observed:

> Probably the basic source of confusion [about affect and emotion] is in the fallacy of reification of concepts. This is the same error which has infested so many of the concepts in psychology, including

that of "mind" itself. Specifically, the error consists in assuming that, because we have a single noun-word, "emotion," something in nature must correspond to it, something as independent, as unique and unchanging, and as readily capable of entering subject-predicate relations with other things. This has led to treating emotion as a separate category or part of behavior, a force and an agent—it is still at the present day spoken of in this way in psychological literature. . . .

Similarly, with regard to the subject of learning, Kendler (1965, pp. 23-24) remarked that:

the construct of learning, whether it be conceived in terms of modifications in cognitive maps or S-R connections, does not refer to an object, thing or entity as suggested by those who are concerned with the question of what is learned. These intervening variables possess no meaning over and above their stated relationships between the independent and the dependent variables. The basic error underlying the problem of what is learned is the assumption that these intervening variables are entities capable of being described and elaborated upon, independent of their operational meaning. The fallacy of reification yields the problem of what is learned. The realization that learning is not a "supra-sensible entity" disposes of it.

Earlier efforts to curb the practice were recorded by Klein (1970, p. 143), who noted that Professor Brett, one of the first and perhaps most scholarly historians of psychology, also called attention to a "persistent fallacy" which, he maintained, continues to characterize "the average mind of the twentieth century." The fallacy results from the consequences of abstracting volitional functions from the total context of mental functions and endowing them with independent status conceived as an isolated entity or faculty of volition. Such reification of volition is analogous to the reification of intelligence.

Perhaps the most well-known instance in psychology of an attempt to sort out the linguistic difficulties associated with the problem is the distinction between intervening variables and hypothetical constructs proposed by MacCorquodale and Meehl (1951). They offered the distinction as a "linguistic convention in the interest of clarity," and noted that perhaps all too frequently

> what [begins] as a name for an intervening variable is finally a name for a "something" which has a host of causal properties. These properties are not made explicit initially, but it is clear that the concept is to be used in an explanatory way which requires that the properties exist. Thus, libido may be introduced by an innocuous definition in terms of the "set of sexual needs" or a "general term for basic strivings." But subsequently we find that certain puzzling phenomena are *deduced* ("explained") by means of the various properties of libido, e.g., that it flows, is dammed up, is converted into something else, tends to regress to earlier channels, adheres to things, makes its "en-

ergy" available to the ego, and so on. . . . [Mac-Corquodale and Meehl, 1951, p. 109]

When expressed and understood literally, and not in a metaphorical sense (cf. Carnap, 1956, p. 22), the concept of libido has been reified.

It is clear from these examples that related to the problem or fallacy of reification is what Beach (1955) has chosen to call the nominal fallacy; Staats and Staats (1963, pp. 13-16) referred to a similar propensity with the phrase "description as pseudoexplanation." The nominal fallacy is "the tendency to confuse naming with explaining," which Beach claimed occurred quite frequently with respect to the concept of instinct. The authors of at least some of the above statements apparently regard the use of reified concepts in explanation as an essential feature of the problem. However, for present purposes, the act of reification, of "mistaking as things entites which are not things," is to be distinguished from the use of reified concepts; their usage is a matter for the problem of explanation to be discussed next.

An outlook on the future of reification in psychology has been stated by Barnett (1967, pp. 196-97) who noted that

being conscious of something . . . is usually taken to imply the existence of a thing or process, called "consciousness"; and this in turn is easily supposed to be an agent which can act on something else. Just as, in the past, the steady temperature of a mammal was attributed to an undefined entity "innate heat," so the intelligence of an animal or human being might be said to be due to, or dependent on, consciousness. Scientific writings contain such reifications; but as knowledge increases, they are gradually, if with difficulty, given up.

However, there is a sense, although a rather special one, in which the act of reification might be tolerated in science, at least in that of physics. Henry Margenau (1950, pp. 57-64) considered it one of the basic "rules of correspondence," a means by which concepts are operationally defined, or objects constructed, in our passage from data to orderly knowledge. "The act of reification of data . . . involves *construction,* construction in accordance with rules" (p. 60). Reification "constitutes the most obvious and therefore the most difficult example of a passage from data to reflective knowledge." It is "an elementary form of a device used under more complex circumstances throughout science." It is a "rule of correspondence, applied automatically," and it apparently owes its "semblance of uniqueness to the *practical* invariability with which it is performed" (p. 61).

"The act of reification is, in fact, the first step taken by our race toward more sophisticated procedures now prevalent in the exact sciences" (p. 62). "The simplest application of the rules [of correspondence] . . . is the act of postulating a *thing* in the face of certain *sensory evidence* . . ." (p. 64). Thus, for Margenau, the act of reification is one of the first, and perhaps most basic, procedures of science. But, despite these considerations, it will probably remain a philosophical problem of psychology for some time to come, perhaps in large part because psychology is concerned with observed events, or behaviors, that do not necessarily need to be constructed into objects as in physics; that is, the observed events of physics seem to require that they be constructed into objects or things whereas the observed events of psychology do not. Hence, psychology will probably continue to regard reification as a practice to be avoided.

It is of some interest to note that reification cannot be a problem for phenomenalism, provided it is consistent, since abstract concepts, constructs, or terms are simply words used to categorize, classify, distinguish, label, stand for, or summarize sensory experience; they cannot be reified since phenomenalism does not require more of its words or abstract concepts than that they be useful for those purposes. However, it does appear to be a special problem for realism since realism requires not only that words be useful, but also, on occasion, that they denote real existing things in the universe independent of an observer. The task for the realist becomes one of distinguishing between at least these two ways in which words are to be used, and, obviously, it is not always clear just how they are used even by those who use them. It would seem, therefore, that the solution to the problem of reification in psychology is a consistent phenomenalism.

5

The Problem of
Explanation

This problem has been introduced by means of the reference in the previous discussion to the nominal fallacy. It seems fairly obvious that a behavioral event is not explained simply by giving it a name. However, if naming is not explanation, then perhaps the meaning of explanation requires some clarification. To a great extent, the problem of explanation in psychology has to do with the manner in which behavioral events are to be explained or with what it means to say that such events have been explained.

There are many conceptions, and perhaps misconceptions, of explanation in psychology. In addition, many of those that can be identified may turn out to be the same when subjected to a closer analysis. Consequently, the ones discussed below are to be thought of as neither mutually exclusive in kind nor exhaustive in number. Rather, they are those that appear most prevalent within the discipline.

The first type of explanation that can be identified in psychology is what might be referred to as explanation by analogy (cf. Reichenbach, 1951, pp. 5-26), and a particularly vivid recent illustration of it within psychology has been described by B.F. Skinner (1969, p 222).

> Primitive origins are not necessarily to be held against an explanatory principle, but the little man (homunculus) is still with us in relatively primitive form. He was recently the hero of a television program called "Gateways to the Mind," one of a series of educational films sponsored by the Bell Telephone Laboratories and written with the help of a distinguished panel of scientists. The viewer learned, from animated cartoons, that when a man's finger was pricked, electrical impulses resembling flashes of lightning run up the afferent nerves and appear on a television screen in the brain. The little man wakes up, sees the flashing screen, reaches out, and pulls a lever. More flashes of lightning go down the nerves to the muscles, which then contract, as the finger is pulled away from the threatening stimulus. The behavior of the homunculus was, of course, not explained. An explanation would presumably require another film. And it, in turn, another.

An explanation of this type appears to relate the event in question to a somewhat more commonly encountered event and emphasizes the similarities between them as though the commonly encountered event, perhaps because it is so common, has no need to be explained. The adequacy of this type of explanation seems to be based on the fact that, when it is used, question asking behavior is likely to cease. If it does not, the result can be an infinite regression of analogies.

For many psychologists, most students of psychology, and nearly all informed laymen with an interest in psychology, to explain a behavioral event is to give the reasons for it. Those reasons are usually mental, and, hence, it could be called a mentalistic, or psychic, explanation. However, Bolles (1967, pp. 2-3) referred to this conception as traditional rationalism.

> The naive and traditional explanation of human behavior is that we act because we have reasons for acting. Because we have free will, our reasons constitute a sufficient account of the whole matter. Such was the common view of the Greek philosophers, and such is the common view of the layman today. Traditional rationalism, of course, receives considerable support from our continuing use of it in our day-to-day contact with people. We hold our fellow man personally responsible as the author of his actions, and society expects him to describe his own actions in terms of intention, awareness, and purpose. We teach our children to use these words by making our transactions with them contingent upon what we consider to be their proper usage. We all do this, even the most behavioristic of us, because that is, in turn, what we have learned to do.

This type of explanation is similar to but somewhat different from the nominal fallacy since the act is not simply named but rather is attributed to an agent such as a desire, want, or wish. An explanation of this type would take the form "He did that because he wanted to," as though the want both served as the agent and accounted for the action. In many cases, such an explanation may be used to justify or defend the action, but however it is used, it does not so much explain behavior as explain it away.

To say that a man does something because he wants to is, for an observer, simply to say that he does it, since what is available for observation is the man doing something and not his want; the want may not even be observed by the man himself because the sensory system through which wants are to be observed has still not been identified. In most cases in which this type of explanation is offered, the effort is expended not so much to explain observed events as to make them consistent with preconceptions about such events.

In addition, however, such an explanation invokes the notion of purpose in behavior, which means essentially that behavior, at least human behavior, is to be explained by its future consequences rather than by those that have occurred in the past (cf. Skinner, 1969, pp. 105-13). It is still enigmatic; how can something that has yet to occur, a future event, possibly influence something that is now occurring, a present event? Moreover, it is quite possible that purpose is less a characteristic of behavior and more a characteristic of whoever observes the behavior; that is, it may be imposed on behavior rather than observed in it. The problem of purpose is another of the philosophical problems of psychology and will receive a more thorough examination later. For now, it is sufficient to point out that the above limitations are what Bolles (1967, pp.

3-5) meant when he said that such explanations are both untestable and teleological.

A third type of explanation in psychology may be called physiological or neural. It is exhibited in the frequently expressed, somewhat wistful, statement made by beginning and intermediate college students that, if only enough were known about physiology, all behavior would be explained. For them, a change in a synaptic connection during learning would account for it. This conception is a form of the mechanistic, physicalistic, or reductionistic explanation described by Bolles (1967, p. 5) as "the doctrine that all natural events have physical causes, and that if we knew enough about physical and mechanical systems we would then be able to explain, at least in principle, all natural phenomena."

Aside from the fact that it introduces the notion of causality, which is the philosophical problem of psychology examined next, this conception appears tc ignore the additional complication that, once the behavior has been explained physiologically, the physiology still remains to be explained (cf. Skinner, 1950). Furthermore, if physiology in turn is to be explained by biochemistry and it by physics, explaining physics poses an enduring problem because there are no sciences left. In other words, this type of explanation leads to a finite regression with one science left unexplained, unless, of course, it is self-explanatory; no one is likely to admit that of physics.

If an incremental change in performance brought about by reinforcement, or learning, is to be explained by a change in a synaptic connection, and the synaptic connection is to be explained by a change in an RNA molecule, and the change in the RNA molecule is to be explained by changes in the various affinities that packets of energy have toward one another, it is not entirely clear how the changes in the affinities are to be explained. If it is the nature of packets of energy to move toward or away from one another depending on their proximity, it might as well be said that it is the nature of reinforcement to produce an incremental change in performance, or, it is the "nature of the beast" to change its performance when it is given food. Clearly, that kind of statement does not explain the change in performance.

A fourth type of explanation is the model, which is a somewhat more sophisticated analogy than that discussed earlier. For example, Marx (1970, p. 11) considered a model

> a conceptual analogue that is used to suggest how empirical research on a problem might best be pursued. That is, the model is a conceptual framework or structure that has been successfully developed in one field and is now applied, primarily as a guide to research and thinking, in some other, usually less well-developed field.

However, there are at least some psychologists, many students of psychology, and many informed laymen who regard a model for complex behavior as an explanation of it; those who develop the model may be particularly prone to do so.

For example, Hinde (1966, p. 34) remarked that the energy models of Freud, McDougall, Lorenz, and Tinbergen "were designed to account for many features of behavior in addition to the phenomena of motivation." In some instances, especially that of Lorenz, the model is developed to the point at which a pictorial representation can be drawn for it. Nevertheless, the diagram of a hydraulic system for motivation, or comparison of the nervous system with a telephone switchboard, or the human brain with an electronic computer, or vicarious trial and error behavior (VTE) with a schematic sow bug (Tolman, 1939) does not explain motivation, the nervous system, the brain, or VTE; they may only make them more familiar. They do not explain because they, in turn, must be explained either by another science or by another model. If the former, there is the problem of a finite regression back to one science left unexplained. If the latter, there is the problem of an infinite regression of models or analogies.

Models, as well as theories, have many uses, at least one of which is explanation. Theoretical explanations are largely deductive and, in that sense, are related to traditional rationalism. However, they also have an empirical, or observational, component and, hence, cannot be equated with rationalism. For example, Hull (1943, p. 3) stated that "an observed event is said to be explained when the proposition expressing it has been logically derived from a set of definitions and postulates coupled with certain observed conditions antecedent to the event." However, "the critical characteristic of scientific theoretical explanation is that it reaches independently through a process of reasoning the same outcome with respect to [secondary] principles as is attained through the process of empirical generalization" (Hull, 1943, p. 5). His point of view was summarized later in the statement:

The main task of science is the isolation of principles which shall be of as general validity as possible. In the methodology whereby scientists have successfully sought this end, two procedures may be distinguished—the empirical and the theoretical. The empirical procedure consists primarily of observation, usually facilitated by experiment. The theoretical procedure, on the other hand, is essentially logical in nature; through its mediation, in conjunction with the employment of the empirical procedure, the range of validity of principles may be explored to an extent quite impossible by the empirical procedure alone. This is notably the case in situations where two or more supposed primary principles are presumably operative simultaneously. The logical procedure yields a statement of the outcome to be expected if the several principles are jointly active as formulated; by comparing deduced or theoretical conclusions with the observed empirical outcomes, it may be determined whether the principles are general enough to cover the situation in question. [Hull, 1943, p. 381]

An explanation of this type involves the determination of whether one or more general principles "cover the situation in question" through the use of empirical and theoretical procedures. In a certain sense, this type of explanation, as well as perhaps all types of explanation, is related to explanation by analogy; the relation appears most evident when it is asserted that the situation in question is similar to those on which the more general principles are based. However, it is distinguishable from explanation by analogy by the fact that, at least in principle, the particular instance in question can be deduced from the more general principles independently of empirical observation, although it may then be confirmed by observation at a later time.

Finally, a sixth type of explanation in psychology is what might be called either empirical explanation or functional explanation. It is the type advocated by both E.R. Guthrie and B.F. Skinner, although it appears to take two somewhat different forms in their writings. The first form is that behavioral events are explained by their laws. For example, Guthrie (1952, p. 9) asserted that "an explanation of any event consists in stating the rule or generalization of which the event is an instance."

> . . . a state of affairs which we may call A (for "antecedent") is followed in a certain proportion (say x percent) of the cases observed by another state of affairs C (for "consequent"). If the law has to do with the degree or quantity of some state instead of merely with its presence or absence it will read: State C is a certain mathematical function of state A, . . . with an observed error of estimate, z.
>
> In such a law both the antecedent and the consequent may be anything whatever, provided that they are observable, describable, and recognizable. The consequent, C, will be something which we are interested in anticipating or predicting; the antecedent, A, will be anything that can conceivably serve as a warning of C. The rule itself, if it is to qualify as scientific, must be the result of observation of cases of A and of C and it should be verified by further observation after it has been formulated. [Guthrie, 1952, p. 10]

The second form of the empirical explanation is that behavioral events are explained by the variables of which they are a function. For example, Skinner (1953, p. 30) stated that:

> The practice of looking inside the organism for an explanation of behavior has tended to obscure the variables which are immediately available for a scientific analysis. These variables lie outside the organism, in its immediate environment and in its environmental history. They have a physical status to which the usual techniques of science are adapted, and they make it possible to explain behavior as other subjects are explained in science. These independent variables are of many sorts and their relations to behavior are often subtle and complex, but we cannot hope to give an adequate account of behavior without analyzing them.

In a later, more explicit statement, he observed that:

> the external variables of which behavior is a function provide for what may be called a causal or functional analysis. We undertake to predict and control the behavior of the individual organism. This is our "dependent variable"—the effect for which we are to find the cause. Our "independent variables"—the causes of behavior—are the external conditions of which behavior is a function. Relations between the two—the "cause-and-effect relationships" in behavior—are the laws of a science. A synthesis of these laws expressed in quantitative terms yields a comprehensive picture

of the organism as a behaving system. [Skinner, 1953, p. 35]

Since quotes are used around "cause-and-effect relationships," it should be emphasized that the phrase is intended in a special sense to be examined in the discussion of the next philosophical problem of psychology. Despite this consideration, both forms of the empirical explanation appear to agree that antecedent events, or independent variables, explain their consequents, or dependent variables, simply by the demonstrated relationships between them. They appear to disagree in the way such explanations are to be formulated. In the former, a behavioral event is explained by stating the "generalization of which the event is an instance." In the latter, the event is explained by stating the "variables of which behavior is a function." In either case, events are explained by an empirical demonstration of how they are related to other events.

There are at least two psychologists who have treated the problem of explanation in psychology in a somewhat different way than that presented above. For example, Marx (1951) differentiated two major types of scientific explanation. They were "the *reductive*—by means of which particular phenomena are functionally related to other phenomena at a different level of description" (p. 14) and "the *constructive*—by means of which the phenomena are described in terms of more abstract, or higher-order, constructs and hypotheses" (p. 15).

When the variables which are used to explain are drawn from observations of a sort arbitrarily assigned to another level of description (for example, the physiological, if organ system functions are directly concerned), the explanation may be considered to be of the reductive type. When the variables are drawn from observations made on the same level of description (the psychological, if behavior is involved), the explanation may be considered to be of the constructive type. In either case the explanation proceeds to a more basic level of description—more basic in the sense that the original behavior data are found to vary systematically as functions of the changes in the other variables introduced. [p. 15]

In a more recent discussion, Turner (1967, p. 178) also identified two major types of explanation in psychology, but they differed somewhat from those of Marx.

In general, events are explained by one of two strategies: by instantiation, or by higher order deductions. In the one case, a particular event is expressed as some particular value of a variable in a general proposition (law); in the other, the law, of which the event is a particular instance, may itself be a hypothesis deducible from within a theory. In neither case does one have the fictionist's freedom to construct just any explanation that aesthetic whim may dictate. Theories, for example, contain laws, theoretical constructs, a logical calculus, and a dictionary. To a large extent the calculus and the theoretical terms are inventions. There may also be a conventional element in the statements of laws and the dictionary. However, in no case are the inventions peremptory. They reflect the factual conceptual traditions of the given science. They also reflect the selective principles of comprehensiveness and simplicity which, at a more subtle level of ontology, are the guides to theoretical evaluation and theoretical convergence.

Obviously, these views on explanation are not necessarily in conflict with those presented earlier, although they may be less comprehensive. For example, the reductive type of explanation discussed by Marx is about the same in kind as the physiological, neural, mechanistic, physicalistic, or reductionistic type of explanation described by Bolles. On the other hand, the constructive type of explanation is analogous to the theoretical explanation of Hull, although it also has some features in common with the reductive type and with both forms of the empirical explanation attributed to Guthrie and Skinner.

Similarly, the type of explanation referred to by Turner as instantiation is almost identical with empirical explanation, whereas his other type of explanation is about the same as theoretical explanation, although it too has features in common with empirical explanation. Hence, these two somewhat different treatments of the problem exclude some other views on explanation that can be found in psychology, and they tend to recombine others in somewhat different ways. Such considerations make it clear that no system of classification for the various views on explanation in psychology is likely to be definitive.

Nowhere in the above discussion does there appear to be a satisfactory way of answering the question "Why?"—For example, "Why does a behavior occur?" For most people, however, it is precisely that question that must be answered when they seek an explanation for a behavioral event. If an answer in the form "it's the nature of the beast" is unacceptable, it is of some interest to examine what an acceptable answer might be.

In most cases, the matter has been dealt with by stating that science cannot answer the question "Why?"; it can only answer the questions "What?" and "How?" since it is primarily descriptive. The question "Why?" appears to require ultimate or absolute causes, and since the truths of science are probable rather than absolute, it cannot answer the question. Nevertheless, people continue to ask the question and expect the various sciences to provide some sort of answer.

It is generally agreed that science cannot provide a statement of the absolute, or certain, causes of an event. But it can state what the probable causes are when the probable causes are the antecedent conditions for the event, or its independent variables. When it is understood that behavior is explained by its causes or antecedent events or independent variables, behavioral science does answer the question "Why?"; it answers the question probably. However, it may well be the case that the why question is finally answered when why-asking behavior ceases, or, when the reply to it, in whatever form explanation may take, is met with a simple "Oh."

6

The Problem of Causality

Remarks by Arthur W. and Carolyn K. Staats (1963, pp. 1-2) help to provide a transition from the problem of explanation to the problem of causality while at the same time illustrating how intimately these problems are related. They observed that:

> especially useful types of observations made by a scientist are those which show the lawful relationships existing between the events in which he is interested and the conditions which determine those events. In everyday language it would be said that the scientist is looking for the "cause" of events.

> The term "cause," however, has come to have philosophical meanings that extend beyond scientific considerations, and today it is preferable to use the term "functional" rather than "causal" in

describing these types of relationships. In any event, the scientific investigator looks for observable events which are related in such a way that if the first event occurs, the second event also occurs. If the first event does not occur, neither does the second. More precisely, the occurrence of the second event may be termed a function of the first. This type of functional relationship constitutes an explanation of the second event; it answers the query concerning why the second event occurred.

For most people, causality is not a problem, and it especially is not a philosophical problem of psychology or any other science. When they say that one event causes another, they simply mean that one event makes the other one take place. The first event is somehow active in bringing about the second one; it produces the second event. Lightning causes thunder, makes it occur, brings it about, or produces it.

However, there are some philosophers, most notably David Hume, for whom the matter is not, or was not, quite so simple; his analysis is referred to, appropriately enough, as the Humean view of causation. Hume (Selby-Bigge, ed., 1888) suggested to his reader that they both cast their "eye on any two objects, which we call cause and effect, and turn them on all sides, in order to find that impression, which produces an idea of such prodigious consequence" (p. 75). What he first observed is that it is not to be sought "in any of the particular *qualities* of the objects" since, regardless of the quality considered, there is at least one

object, that is not possest of it, and yet falls under the denomination of cause or effect. And indeed there is nothing existent, either externally or internally, which is not to be consider'd either as a cause or an effect; tho' tis plain there is no one quality, which universally belongs to all beings, and gives them a title to that denomination. [p. 75]

It is not observed in the qualities of objects; it is not a quality of objects. Any object or event may be, depending on the circumstances of observation, either cause or effect. Consequently, the idea "of causation must be deriv'd from some *relation* among objects." In fact, he finds it derived from several relations among objects.

The first relation is contiguity. Hume (Selby-Bigge, ed., 1888) observed:

that whatever objects are consider'd as causes or effects, are *contiguous;* and that nothing can operate in a time or place, which is ever so little remov'd from those of its existence. Tho' distant objects may sometimes seem productive of each other, they are commonly found upon examination to be link'd by a chain of causes, which are contiguous among themselves, and to the distant objects; and when in any particular instance we cannot discover this connexion, we still presume it to exist.

[The second relation] is that of PRIORITY of time in the cause before the effect . . . we may establish the relation of priority by a kind of inference of reasoning. 'Tis an establish'd maxim both in natural and moral philosophy, that an object, which exists for any time in its full perfection without producing another, is not its sole cause; but is assisted by some other principle, which pushes it from its state of inactivity, and makes it exert that energy, of which it was secretly possest. Now if any cause may be perfectly co-temporary with its effect, 'tis certain, according to this maxim, that they must all be so; since any one of them, which retards its operation for a single moment, exerts not itself at that very individual time, in which it might have operated; and therefore is no proper cause. The consequence of this wou'd be no less than the destruction of that succession of causes, which we observe in the world; and indeed, the utter annihilation of time. For if one cause were co-temporary with its effect, and this effect with *its* effect, and so on, 'tis plain there wou'd be no such thing as succession, and all objects must be co-existent.

[However] an object may be contiguous and prior to another, without being consider'd as its cause. There is a NECESSARY CONNEXION to be taken into consideration; and that relation is of much greater importance, than [the other two] . . . in advancing we have insensibly discover'd a new relation betwixt cause and effect, when we least expected it, and were entirely employ'd upon another subject. This relation is their CONSTANT CONJUNCTION. Contiguity and succession are not sufficient to make us pronounce any two objects to be cause and effect, unless we perceive, that these two relations are preserv'd in several instances. . . . [Constant conjunction] implies no more than this, that like objects have always been plac'd in like relations of contiguity and succession.

As our senses shew us in the one instance two bodies, or motions, or qualities in certain relations of succession and contiguity; so our memory presents us only with a multitude of instances, wherein we always find like bodies, motions, or qualities in like relations. From the mere repetition of any past impression, even to infinity, there never will arise any new original idea, such as that of a necessary connexion; and the number of impressions has in this case no more effect than if we confin'd ourselves to one only . . . and having found, that after the discovery of the constant conjunction of any objects, we always draw an inference from one object to another, we shall now examine the nature of that inference, and of the transition from the impression to the idea. Perhaps 'twill appear in the end, that the necessary connexion depends on the inference, instead of the inference's depending on the necessary connexion. [pp. 75-88]

The necessary connection is more a characteristic of the observer than it is of observed events. The relation of necessary connection becomes a matter of an observed constant conjunction between those events referred to as causes and those referred to as effects. And since a constant conjunction is practically equivalent to invariant contiguity and priority, Hume's analysis reveals only two observed relations between events that provide the basis for asserting that one causes the other; they are an invariable contiguity and priority or succession. When two events are always contiguous, with one always prior to the other, the first is said to be the cause of the second. The object or event referred to as the cause never follows the effect and, hence, priority is required to preserve the direction of the relationship. It is important to note that these relations are analyzed out of sense experience and not necessarily out of the events themselves. In short, cause and effect may operate less without, than they do within, the observer.

This interpretation is apparently consistent with that by Bolles (1967), who concluded:

Hume's skeptical epistemology led him to the realization that the best evidence we can ever obtain [about causation] is that two events invariably occur together, one preceding the other, always in the same order, and neither occurring alone. The imputation of causation, the abstract conception that the prior event necessitates the subsequent event, is an inference which goes beyond the evidence. There may be such a thing as physical or material causation, of course, but we can never be sure whether nature operates mechanistically since all we can know is the successive experience of successive events. [p. 7]

By contrast, the conclusion reached by Boring (1957a, p. 192) from his review of the analysis is that causation may be viewed simply as correlation. However, correlated events may not only be contiguous, they may also be contemporary, or "co-temporary," in the sense that they occur at the same time. But cotemporary events are apparently specifically excluded by Hume from consideration as causal events, and consequently the conclusion that causation is correlation does not appear to be supported by direct reference to the analysis. The priority relation may be more important than was even realized by Hume, since not only must events be invariably contiguous, but also one must always be prior to the other before we are likely to consider one as the cause and the other as the effect.

Related to the interpretation by Boring is one by Riechenbach (1951):

> Since repetition is all that distinguishes the causal law from a mere coincidence, the meaning of causal relation consists in the statement of an exceptionless repetition—it is unnecessary to assume that it means more. The idea that a cause is connected with its effect by a sort of hidden string, that the effect is forced to follow the cause, is anthropomorphic in its origin and is dispensable: *if-then always* is all that is meant by a causal relation. If the theater would always shake when an explosion is visible on the screen, then there would be causal relationship. We do not mean anything else when we speak of causality. [p. 158]

A slightly different interpretation has been offered by B.F. Skinner (1953), who stated:

> The terms "cause" and "effect" are no longer widely used in science. They have been associated with so many theories of the structure and operation of the universe that they mean more than scientists want to say. The terms which replace them, however, refer to the same factual core. A "cause" becomes a "change in an independent variable" and an "effect" a "change in a dependent variable." The old "cause and effect connection"

becomes a "functional relation." The new terms
do not suggest *how* a cause causes its effect; they
merely assert that different events tend to occur
together in a certain order. This is important, but it
is not crucial. There is no particular danger in using
"cause" and "effect" in an informal discussion if we
are always ready to substitute their more exact
counterparts. [p. 23]

The interpretation of cause and effect as correlation was reconciled with the interpretation of it as a
functional relation by Feigl (1953), who remarked:

The crude concepts of cause and effect connote
of course the generally accepted definition in
terms of the temporal precedence of *cause*. But an
equally well established usage seems to prevail
even if the two events (factors, processes) are
contemporaneous. Since the purely mathematical
concept of the "independent variable" is obviously arbitrary (to any function there is its in-
verse), the empirical meaning of "independent"
and "dependent" variable must lie somewhere
else. Perhaps what we mean here by "cause"
(independent variable) and "effect" (dependent
variable) simply hinges upon which of the variables are open to active control, accessible to
intervention. [p. 417]

Finally, Turner (1967) observed:

For the radical empiricist, the end of the
odyssey is Humean skepticism. Indeed, explanation and causal analysis can penetrate no further

than the inevitable barriers of contiguity. We are often told that correlation does not mean causation, but as good Humeans, we can discount the argument by introducing certain space and time provisos with respect to stipulating the antecedents and consequents in a causal sequence. Correlation may not be causation; but causation *is* correlation unless, of course, we leave the domain of pure empirics—in which case it would be as well that we drop the language of causality altogether. [p. 271]

All of these authors appear to agree that causation is correlation, but it is correlation with a difference. That is, it is not simply the relationship between two dependent variables but, rather, the relationship between an independent variable and a dependent variable where the independent one may be prior to or contemporaneous with the dependent variable. In short, they all seem to agree that a causal relationship is a functional relationship.

Behavioral science will probably retain, and find useful, the concept of causality in the sense of a functional relationship. However, it could equally well conclude with Bertrand Russell (1953) that "the law of causality . . . like much that passes muster among philosophers, is a relic of a bygone age, surviving, like the monarchy, only because it is erroneously supposed to do no harm" (p. 387).

7

The Problem of Theory

Those who are only casually acquainted with this problem may suppose that a theorist publishes his theory, or makes it public in some other way, because he believes it is a true statement about the nature of the universe or some aspect of it; the theorist himself may believe that his theory is true. That is, casual acquaintance with the problem may lead to the view that a theorist theorizes because he is convinced that he knows something either not known by anyone else or known by only a few, and he wants to share his knowledge with a wider audience. Thus, for example, Sigmund Freud published his theory of human motivation because he believed it was true that most humans do most of the things they do from sexual motives, and he wanted others to know about it in case they had not discovered it for themselves. In other words, for most people the problem of theory in psychology is whether it is true or false.

However, it does not take long for the student of psychology to learn that, on the basis of what psychologists now claim to know about theory, theories are neither true nor false; they are only more or less useful, or fruitful, perhaps for integrating observations already performed and for making predictions subject to observational test. For example, Turner (1967, p. 176) remarked:

> Theories are useful and they are "contextually true," but only to the extent they generate well-confirmed hypotheses. Their extension is empirically determined and provisional. They make no claim to an absolute truth status that would enable us to prejudge the world and retire from the ontological quest.

Theories can be neither true nor false because the methodology of the science provides a basis only for the assertion of statements, including theories, that simply are probable, and since they are probable, they cannot be absolutely true or certain. A somewhat different illustration of this point is provided by Marx (1970, p. 15), who observed that "in real scientific life most theories contribute not by being right but by being wrong. In other words, scientific advance in theory as well as experiment tends to be built upon the successive correction of many errors, both small and large. Thus the popular notion that a theory must be right to be useful is incorrect."

A further complication is that, even though such

statements might in fact be certain, they cannot be known to be certain because one more observation, at least in principle, always can be made immediately after the last one. The process of observation is never complete; it could continue ad infinitum, and perhaps ad absurdum. This complication is illustrated in the remark by Feigl (1970, p. 12) that "Einstein's deep conviction of the basic determinism—at 'rock bottom'—of nature is shared by very few theoretical physicists today. There may be no rock bottom; moreover there is no criterion that would tell us that we have reached rock bottom (if indeed we had!)."

It would be misleading to say that all psychologists who have written on the subject agree that the problem of theory in psychology is what it does rather than what it is; many attempts have been made to say what it is. In addition, while most of them might admit that utility, or usefulness, is its major contribution to the conduct of the science or "doing psychology," not all would support the assertion that it is useful in the sense of integration and prediction. Such considerations are about the topic of theory per se and have come to be regarded as "meta-theory" or theory of theory in both philosophy and psychology.

Discussions of meta-theory may be found in Marx (1970), Madsen (1968), and Bolles (1967), who, in turn, are somewhat indebted to Koch (1959), Estes, et al. (1954), and Spence (1944), to name only a few of those psychologists who have helped to shape current metatheory in psychology. They, in turn, owe a debt to those philosophers of science, especially the logical analysts and empiricists, who profited from but nevertheless survived the influence of logical positivism on both philosophy and science. These sources are a useful introduction to some of the more complex aspects of this problem.

For now, it is sufficient to note that the subject of meta-theory has not been exhausted in this rather brief reference to it and that unanimity by no means prevails. There are a number of meta-theories in psychology today. The classical, and perhaps most extreme, ones are those of C.L. Hull (1943) and B.F. Skinner (1938), although their later comments on the subject rendered them less extreme than is commonly thought (cf. Hull, 1952; Skinner, 1969).

As is well known, Hull (1943) aspired to develop what has been called a hypothetico-deductive behavior theory analogous to the type of theory developed, especially by Isaac Newton, in the physical sciences. In the first section of the final chapter of *Principles of Behavior*, entitled "The Nature of Scientific Theory," Hull asserted:

> Scientific theory in its ideal form consists of a hierarchy of logically deduced propositions which parallel all the observed empirical relationships composing a science. This logical structure is derived from a relatively small number of self-consistent primary principles called postulates, when taken in conjunction with relevant antecedent conditions. The behavior sciences have been slower than the physical sciences to attain this systematic status, in part because of their inherent complexity, in part because of the action of the oscillation principle, but also in part because of the greater persistence of anthropomorphism.
>
> Empirical observation, supplemented by

shrewd conjecture, is the main source of the primary principles or postulates of a science. Such formulations, when taken in various combinations together with relevant antecedent conditions, yield inferences or theorems, of which some may agree with the empirical outcome of the conditions in question, and some may not. Primary propositions yielding logical deductions which consistently agree with the observed empirical outcome are retained, whereas those which disagree are rejected or modified. As the sifting of this trial-and-error process continues, there gradually emerges a limited series of primary principles whose joint implications are progressively more likely to agree with relevant observations. Deductions made from these surviving postulates, while never absolutely certain, do at length become highly trustworthy. This is in fact the present status of the primary principles of the major physical sciences. [Hull, 1943, pp. 381-82]

Aside from more explicitly introducing the problem of anthropomorphism, this excerpt reveals the hypothetico-deductive nature of scientific theory, and theory construction, as it was understood by Hull. A theory begins to emerge by way of hypotheses deduced from primary principles or postulates based on empirical observation and perhaps shrewd conjecture. These hypotheses, in turn, are rejected or retained depending on observational confirmation. The process results in "a hierarchy of logically deduced propositions which parallel all the observed empirical relationships composing a science," that is, a theory.

In addition, however, the activity of theorizing requires the use of concepts, or constructs, to link preceding or antecedent events with those that follow or consequent events. For example, Hull continued immediately after the above statement with the following proposition:

> Scientific theories are mainly concerned with dynamic situations, i.e., with the consequent events or conditions which, with the passage of time, will follow from a given set of antecedent events or conditions. The concrete activity of theorizing consists in the manipulation of a limited set of symbols according to the rules expressed in the postulates (together with certain additional rules which make up the main substance of logic) in such a way as to span the gap separating the antecedent conditions or states from the subsequent ones. Some of the symbols represent observable and measurable elements or aggregates of the situation, whereas others represent presumptive intervening processes not directly subject to observation. The latter are theoretical constructs. All well-developed sciences freely employ theoretical constructs wherever they prove useful, sometimes even sequences or chains of them. The scientific utility of logical constructs consists in the mediation of valid deductions; this in turn is absolutely dependent upon every construct, or construct chain, being securely anchored both on the antecedent and on the consequent side to conditions or events which are directly observable. If possible, they should also be measurable. [Hull, 1943, pp. 282-83]

At the other extreme of classical meta-theory is the one by Skinner. The relevant comments on the subject of meta-theory by Skinner are about a system rather than a theory. However, since systems frequently are equated with theories, his views are presented here as a meta-theory.

In the opening paragraphs to the second chapter of *The Behavior of Organisms*, Skinner (1938, pp. 44-45) stated:

> So far as scientific method is concerned, the system set up in the preceding chapter may be characterized as follows. It is positivistic. It confines itself to description rather than explanation. Its concepts are defined in terms of immediate observations and are not given local or physiological properties. A reflex is not an arc, a drive is not the state of a center, extinction is not the exhaustion of a physiological substance or state. Terms of this sort are used merely to bring together groups of observations, to state uniformities, and to express properties of behavior which transcend single instances. They are not hypotheses, in the sense of things to be proved or disproved, but convenient representations of things already known. As to hypotheses, the system does not require them—at least in the usual sense.
>
> It is often objected that a positivistic system offers no incentive to experimentation. The hypothesis, even the bad hypothesis, is said to be justified by its effect in producing research (presumably even bad research), and it is held or implied that some such device is usually needed. This is an historical question about the motivation

of human behavior. There are doubtless many men whose curiosity about nature is less than their curiosity about the accuracy of their guesses, but it may be noted that science does in fact progress without the aid of this kind of explanatory prophecy. Much can be claimed for the greater efficiency of the descriptive system, when it is once motivated.

Granted, however, that such a system does possess the requisite moving force, it may still be insisted that a merely descriptive science must be lacking in direction. A fact is a fact; and the positivistic system does not seem to prefer one to another. Hypotheses are declared to solve this problem by directing the choice of facts (what directs the choice of hypotheses is not often discussed), and without them a distinction between the useful and the useless fact is said to be impossible. This is a narrow view of a descriptive science. The mere accumulation of uniformities is not a science at all. It is necessary to organize facts in such a way that a simple and convenient description can be given, and for this purpose a structure or system is required. The exigencies of a satisfactory system provide all the direction in the acquisition of facts that can be desired. Although natural history has set the pattern for the collection of isolated bits of curious behavior, there is no danger that a science of behavior will reach that level.

It is understandable how this rather lengthy and frequently quoted passage could be used as evidence that Skinner espoused an atheoretical position. It is certainly clear that he opposed some of the accepted views on theory that were current at the time he wrote. Nevertheless, terms were used "to bring together groups of observations, to state uniformities, and to express properties of behavior which transcend single instances." In addition, it was "necessary to organize facts in such a way that a single and convenient description" could be given, "and for this purpose a structure or system" was required. In other words, the major emphasis was upon integration of particular observed instances of behavior into more general expressions for them, which illustrates the inductive nature of his views on meta-theory. They contrast with those of Hull in which particular instances were inferred from general statements and then subjected to some sort of observational test, which illustrates the deductive nature of Hull's views on meta-theory; for Hull, the major emphasis was apparently upon prediction, although integration was by no means ignored.

Thus, while it can be argued that Skinner was atheoretical in the sense in which theory was then generally understood, it cannot be said that he was atheoretical in the sense in which he had come to understand that term. His views, at least as much as those of any other psychologist, also have helped to shape current meta-theory in psychology. Perhaps in large part because of that influence, historical hindsight has revealed at least four major kinds of theory, or theories of theory, within psychology today (cf. Marx, 1970). They have been classified by the manner in which they are constructed, and according to that classification, Skinner's is an inductive theory whereas Hull's is a deductive theory; the two that remain are the model and the functional types of theories.

Theory

According to Sigmund Koch (1959), the conception of theory as something to be produced or constructed characterized what could be referred to as an "Age of Theory" in psychology; both Hull and Skinner contributed their early views on theory during that period. Apparently, this interpretation has persisted inot the present since it provides the basis for the classification of the four meta-theories examined by Marx (1970).

Whatever else it may be, theory for Marx involves some sort of dynamic interplay between a system of symbols, on the one hand, and sense experience, observations, or data, on the other; the extent to which they interact results in the four different types of meta-theories. For example, the model involves almost no interaction between the system of symbols and observations. It is simply a kind of analogy, which might include a pictorial representation, that is used to provide suggestions for research in some problem area. However, the results of that research are not used, in turn, to modify the model; there is only a single direction of influence from model to data but none in return to the model.

On the other hand, a deductive theory such as Hull's clearly represents a two-way interaction between the system of symbols and observations. Deductions or predictions from the logically related propositions of the theory are derived and then tested under controlled conditions of observations, and in turn, the propositions are modified either in whole or in part by the results of those tests. This type of theory is similar to a functional theory except that the functional theory is narrower in scope. Whereas a deductive theory might aim toward universality, in the sense that it is intended to apply, for example, to the behavior of organisms and might require rather lengthy deductive inferences from general propositions to specific statements that can be observationally tested, a functional theory is more closely "tied to the data." It may be restricted to some behavior of some organisms and a special kind of problem with rather short-term inferences from theory to data and from data to theory. Nevertheless, the interplay between theory and data prevails; the theory suggests data, and the data suggest theory. For Marx, most of what passes for theory in psychology today is in this functional mode of theory construction.

Finally, an inductive theory such as Skinner's is similar to the model in that, once again, there is almost no interplay between symbols and data. However, the direction of influence is exactly counter to that in the model; the movement is from data to theory, but there is no return from theory to data. The theory is useful, but it is not used to predict. It is used to integrate; it organizes or summarizes observations or data and that is all.

These four modes of formal theory construction are not necessarily exhaustive, but they do serve as focal types for which examples can be found within psychology at the present time. Significantly, they are defined less by what they are than by how they are constructed or, it might be said, by the contribution they make to the conduct of the science. All four of them are heuristic, or useful in stimulating research, but they are useful in somewhat different ways. A model may help to organize, or integrate, some problem area that is otherwise unorganized and may simply suggest observations that might be performed in that area. Both deductive and functional theories not only provide some formal organization, or integration, of observations that already have been performed, but they also allow deduction of hypotheses, or predictions, for observational testing. Finally, an inductive theory simply summarizes, or integrates, observations that have accumulated through the use of the methods of science. No one of these theories is necessarily more important or significant than any of the others; all are of some consequence to the extent that they enable psychologists to learn more about the behavior of organisms.

8

Laws and Principles

This problem is very closely related to the problem of theory but may be treated independently of it. The problem is also related to explanation and causality as illustrated in the remarks quoted earlier from Staats and Staats (1963) with respect to all three problems. For a great many people, the laws of a science like the laws of a society are to be obeyed by the events they describe, and principles are something by which to live; the latter are guides to conduct whether in science or in society. For that matter, there are a good many scientists who use the term *law* as though the events described by a law are in turn governed by it, whereas the term *principle* refers to some basic assumption that guides the conduct of inquiry.

However, just as with the problem of metaphysics, it does not now seem possible to know whether events are governed by their laws or simply described by them, since to know whether they are either governed or described would seem to require access to a real world, which, if known, could be known at all only by means of sense experience. And, if a real world can be known only through sense experience, then it may be that what is known is sense experience and not a real world. Consequently, as with many of the philosophical problems of psychology, the problem of laws and principles is the problem of metaphysics, or ontology, in a somewhat different form.

There are other scientists, especially behavioral scientists or psychologists, for whom the problem of laws and principles is a semantic or, perhaps more accurately, syntactic one; for them, the problem is what is meant by the terms *laws* and *principles*. For example, Kaplan (1964, p. 84) introduced his chapter on "Laws" with the statement that:

> Generalizations of a number of different kinds play a part in the process of science, and perform a number of correspondingly different functions. The outcome of every successful inquiry is usually thought of as being either particular or general; if particular, it is said to have established a "fact," and if general, a "law." Whatever other generalizations are formulated in the course of inquiry are thought of as being only laws in the making. A hypothesis, for instance, is conceived to differ from a law only in not yet having been sufficiently well established.
>
> [However,] laws are not generalizations at which we arrive after we have established the facts: they play a part in the process of determin-

ing what the facts are. Indeed, we may without a vicious circularity accept some datum as a fact because it conforms to the very law for which it counts as another confirming instance, and reject an allegation of fact because it is already excluded by law. [Kaplan, 1964, p. 89]

Thus, according to Kaplan, the usual meaning of the term *laws* is that they are general expressions of which facts are particular instances, and not only are there differences between facts and laws but they, in turn, differ from hypotheses, although none is entirely independent of the others. Later, he concluded that laws cannot be understood except by the way in which they function in science, and they do not have a single function. Thus, his view of law might be regarded as either functional, instrumental, or, perhaps, pragmatic; laws are what laws do.

Kaplan may be classified as a behavioral scientist or at least a philosopher of behavioral science. However, there are other behavioral scientists, especially psychologists, who view the matter of laws somewhat differently. For example, Melvin H. Marx rather consistently has held to an alternative formulation over the years (cf. Marx, 1951, 1963, 1970). In one source (Marx, 1963, p. 7), he stated that, if philosophical and logical issues were ignored, a scientific law could be

defined as a statement of regular, predictable relationship among empirical variables. Sometimes, especially in older usages, the term law means a strongly established theoretical or abstract principle. However, it is increasingly being used to refer to the basic regularities observed in natural phenomena and thus typically to represent the descriptive and the empirical, rather than the abstracted and the inferred, properties of data. (The term data refers to the recorded results of observations, often but not necessarily in quantitative form; the term variable refers to a factor or condition involved in the investigation—to a class of objects or events, or to a class of properties of objects or events).

Laws may sometimes be confused with principles, at least in older usage, but according to Marx psychologists are coming more and more to regard laws as descriptive, empirical statements of orderly relationships between measurable variables. Apparently, it is only occasionally that they perhaps mistakenly assert that laws govern the events they describe.

Another psychologist concerned with the laws of behavioral science, and one who provided a rather exhaustive analysis of the various kinds of laws in psychology, was Kenneth W. Spence (cf. Spence, 1944, 1956, 1963). For example, he stated:

Like every other scientist, the psychologist is interested in discovering and formulating the relations or laws holding among these different classes of variables (response, stimulus, and organic). The several types of laws with which psychologists have been concerned are as follows: (I) $R=f(R)$; (II) $R=f(S)$: (III) $O=f(S)$; (IV) $R=f(O)$.

The first class, $R=f(R)$ laws, describes relations between different attributes or properties of behavior; they tell us which behavior traits are associated. This type of law is investigated extensively in the fields of intelligence and personality testing, and the laws that have been discovered have formed the basis of much of our technology in the areas of guidance, counseling, and clinical diagnosis. These empirical R-R relations also form the starting point for the theoretical constructs of the factor analysts. Beginning with the intercorrelations among a large number of test (response) scores these theorists have attempted by means of their mathematical methods to discover a minimum set of hypothetical factors that could account for the variance in the behavioral measures. The so-called field theory of Lewin . . . was also concerned primarily with this R-R type of law, his theoretical concepts being introduced in terms of response variables and eventually returning to other response variables.

The second class of laws, R=f(S), relates response measures as the dependent variable to the determining environmental conditions. There are really two subclasses of laws here; one relating to the environmental events of the present and the second to events of the past. The first subclass includes the traditional laws of psychophysics, perception, reaction time, and emotions. These laws describe how behavior varies with changes in the present physical stimulus. The theories that have been investigated by this kind of law are primarily of the reductionistic type, involving hypotheses as to the nature of the underlying neurophysiological mediating mechanisms.

Insofar as the behavior at any moment is a function of environmental events that occurred prior to the time of observation one is dealing with

laws of the second subclass. The most familiar
instance of this kind of relation is represented by
the so-called learning curve which relates the
response variable to previous environmental
events of a specified character. Laws of primary
and secondary motivation are other examples that
fall in this group. These laws have provided the
starting point of most theories of learning, although some learning theories have been initiated
on the basis of neurophysiological laws.

A survey of the research literature since the
beginning of experimental psychology will reveal
the extraordinary extent to which the interests of
psychologists have turned more and more to the
investigation of laws of the first and second class.
Less and less interest has been shown in the third
and fourth class of relations which involve, as one
of the members, physiological and anatomical
variables. This trend was apparent even in the
early developments in psychophysics. [Spence,
1956, pp. 16-17].

It is of some importance to note that, for Spence,
psychologists not only formulate but also discover the
laws of their science, which indicates once more that at
least some psychologists have solved the problem of
metaphysics, or ontology, in favor of realism. Despite
that consideration, laws for him are relations, empirically established relations, between three major classes
of variables, although interest has narrowed over the
years to just two of them, stimulus and response; these
two major classes of variables may be thought of as
independent and dependent variables, respectively.

For example, in their discussion of laws in

psychology, Staats and Staats (1963, pp. 16-18) remarked:

> Explanation in psychology, as in other sciences, is developed upon the basis of systematic observation. That is, when systematic observation of some phenomenon has been made, the second stage in the development of a science may begin: the search for the cause of the phenomenon, or, more accurately, the specification of some independently observed prior event to which it is related.
>
> The stuff out of which the lawful relationships are found are the *observations* of the events in which the scientist is interested and the *independent observations* of the conditions that determine these events. In order to explain an event, then, something more than observing and describing similar events must be done. The *antecedent* conditions under which the event will occur must be known, as well as those conditions under which it will not occur. That is, the relationships between the event of concern and the events determining it must be established. [p. 16]
>
> Having found a lawful relationship between two events, one preceding the other in time—in commensense terms a "cause"—two powerful products of science may be obtained. First, if the occurrence of event$_1$ is reliably followed by (lawfully related to) event$_2$, knowledge of event$_1$ gives knowledge of what event$_2$ will be. [p. 17]

In addition to the power of prediction, empirical laws may also yield control. Interest in a particular natural event is often accompanied by an interest in influencing or controlling its occurrence. Now, if there is a lawful relationship between $event_1$ and $event_2$, the second event can be predicted from the first. Moreover, if $event_1$ can be manipulated so that it either does or does not occur, then the control of $event_2$ is achieved. [p. 18]

In the discussion that followed these remarks, $event_1$ was called the independent variable as well as the antecedent condition or event, whereas $event_2$ was called the dependent variable as well as the consequent condition or event.

In general, an independent variable in psychology is some environmental event to which an experimenter can assign certain measurable values by means of a direct manipulation of it; it is frequently referred to as a stimulus (S). On the other hand, a dependent variable is some measure of behavior that can be manipulated only indirectly by means of control over an independent variable to which it may be related; such a variable is frequently referred to as a response (R). Staats and Staats were concerned especially with the ways in which S is related to R, as well as with how one R is related to another R. As with Spence, they were mainly interested in S-R and R-R laws, which, from their discussion, could be interpreted as the lawful relations between either one independent and one dependent variable or two dependent variables, respectively; the former are sometimes referred to as functional laws and the latter as correlational.

Apparently, these two types of laws have somewhat different distinguishing characteristics and products (cf. Staats and Staats, 1963, pp. 20-26). An S-R law is a functional relationship between at least one independent and one dependent variable. It has two products: prediction and control. Such a law can be used to predict from some value of S what some value of R might be, but also, since S is an independent variable, R can be controlled by manipulating S; this type of law appears to be about as close as contemporary science can come to a "causal" law.

On the other hand, an R-R law is a correlation between at least two response measures or dependent variables. It has only one product: prediction. Such a law can be used to predict from some value of one R what some value of the other R might be, but since neither is an independent variable, control of one by means of the other is not possible. Apparently, it is with these two types of laws that events are explained in contemporary psychology, or at least that appears to be the hope of those who have discussed the matter of explanation in psychology most recently.

The title of the book by Staats and Staats was *Complex Human Behavior: A Systematic Extension of Learning Principles.* Since the subtitle contained the term *principles,* an examination of their views on principles appears to be in order at this point in the discussion of laws and principles. However, they do not state precisely what they mean by that term except by way of quotations from B.F. Skinner and K.W. Spence. The former makes reference to statements about statements and the latter to statements about laws. In both cases, it would appear that the meaning of the term *principle* is that it is a statement about laws or a generalization across laws, which seems to be the way in which Staats and Staats use the term in the remainder of their discussion.

The term *principle* has appeared in the title of a good many other textbooks in psychology. One of the earliest was *The Principles of Psychology* by William James (ca. 1890). In the preface to the first volume of that two-volume work, he remarked:

I have kept close to the point of view of natural science throughout the book. Every natural science assumes certain data uncritically, and declines to challenge the elements between which its own 'laws' obtain, and from which its own deductions are carried on. Psychology, the science of finite individual minds, assumes as its data (1) *thoughts and feelings,* and (2) *a physical world* in time and space with which they coexist and which (3) *they know.* Of course these data themselves are discussable; but the discussion of them (as of other elements) is called metaphysics and falls outside the province of this book. This book, assuming that thoughts and feelings exist and are vehicles of knowledge, thereupon contends that psychology when she has ascertained the empirical correlation of the various sorts of thought or feeling with definite conditions of the brain, can go no farther—can go no farther, that is, as a natural science. If she goes farther she becomes metaphysical. All attempts to *explain* our phenomenally given thoughts as products of deeper-lying entities (whether the latter be named 'Soul,' 'Trancendental Ego,' 'Ideas,' or 'Elementary Units of

Consciousness') are metaphysical. This book consequently rejects both the associationist and the spiritualist theories; and in this strictly positivistic point of view consists the only feature of it for which I feel tempted to claim originality. Of course this point of view is anything but ultimate. Men must keep thinking; and the data assumed by psychology, just like those assumed by physics and the other natural sciences, must some time be overhauled. The effort to overhaul them clearly and thoroughly is metaphysics; but metaphysics can only perform her task well when distinctly conscious of its great extent. Metaphysics fragmentary, irresponsible, and half-awake, and unconscious that she is metaphysical, spoils two good things when she injects herself into a natural science. And it seems to me that the theories both of a spiritual agent and of associated 'ideas' are, as they figure in the psychology-books, just such metaphysics as this. Even if their results be true, it would be as well to keep them, *as thus presented,* out of psychology as it is to keep the results of idealism out of physics.

I have therefore treated our passing thoughts as integers, and regarded the mere laws of their coexistence with brain-states as the ultimate laws of our science. The reader will in vain seek for any closed system in the book. It is mainly a mass of descriptive details, running out into queries which only a metaphysics alive to the weight of her task can hope successfully to deal with. That will perhaps be centuries hence; and meanwhile the best mark of health that a science can show is this unfinished-seeming front. [James, 1950, pp. v-vii]

Thus, it would appear that, for James, principles are the ultimate laws of a science.

However, his views on principles, and many other matters, were not uncomplicated. For example, he later referred to principles as propositions of fact and apparently contrasted them with postulates of rationality or metaphysical principles, such as the principle of causality, as well as esthetic and moral principles (cf. James, 1950, pp. 670-72).

The conception of principles as the ultimate laws of a science is not necessarily incompatible with the conception that they are propositions of fact. And his propositions of fact, or principles of psychology, included: habit; attention; conception; discrimination and comparison; association; time, object, space, and reality perception; memory; sensation; imagination; reasoning; and will. Not all of them were based on hard empirical evidence, and none of them are necessarily principles of psychology today. However, many of them still are subject to active experimentation and consideration by contemporary psychologists.

The term *principle* also appeared in the title of what now might be called another classic work in psychology by Clark L. Hull (1943); it was *Principles of Behavior: An Introduction to Behavior Theory*. In the preface to it, Hull stated that it "attempts to present in an objective, systematic manner the primary, or fundamental, molar principles of behavior. It has been written on the assumption that all behavior, individual and social, moral and immoral, normal and psychopathic, is generated from the same primary laws" (p. v). Several pages later in his definition of theory, primary principles were referred to as postulates and compared to the axioms of geometry. Thus, for Hull, principles were not simply generalizations across laws, or the ultimate laws of a science, or propositions of fact, but those things and more, especially as they entered into the deduction of secondary principles.

The term also has appeared in the more recent *Principles of Psychology: A Systematic Text in the Science of Behavior* by Fred S. Keller and William N. Schoenfeld (1950). In the preface to their work, the authors asserted:

This book is a new kind of introduction to psychology. It is different in that it represents for the first time a point of view that is coming to guide the thinking and research of an active group of psychologists in this country. The members of this group are mainly experimentalists, laboratory workers, who spend much of their time in observing and measuring the behavior of organisms—rats, dogs, guinea-pigs, apes, pigeons, and, of course, human beings. They are unflaggingly on the lookout for fundamental principles of behavior—principles that hold true for the white rat as well as the college student, for the dog in the laboratory harness as well as for the patient on the psychoanalyst's couch, for the tribal savage as well as the sophisticated product of our own culture. Already they have discovered some of these principles and have brought them together in the beginnings of scientific theory. Other principles are, at present, only suspected, and the search goes on at an ever faster pace. In this book, we try to tell about the ones of which we are certain; we describe some of the research they are based on; and we point out the way in which they may be organized to give a meaningful picture of human conduct. [Keller and Schoenfeld, 1950, p. vii]

Later, in the first paragraph of their first chapter, they also remarked that "the purpose of this text is three-fold: (1) to acquaint you with a number of well-established psychological principles; (2) to show you how these principles are related, one to the other; and (3) to suggest how you may apply them in the analysis of everyday human activity" (Keller and Schoenfeld, 1950, p. 1). On the next page, they asserted:

Our approach is biological, experimental, and systematic. *Biological,* in that our basic principles will often be drawn from the study of animal behavior, and will be found to apply at various evolutionary levels; *experimental,* in that these principles will be derived, not from casual observation or untested opinion, but from laboratory studies in which the important factors are isolated and varied in such a manner as to permit scientific lawfulness to be discovered; and *systematic,* in that the interrelation of experimental facts will be one of our major concerns. [Keller and Schoenfeld, 1950, p. 2]

It would seem, therefore, that these authors use the term principle in much the same way as Staats and Staats use it, but there does not appear to be unanimity at least among psychologists on precisely what is meant by either the term *principle* or, for that matter, the term *law;* the former has appeared in the titles of many other textbooks in psychology with no clear statement of how it is to be understood.

Perhaps this lack of unanimity has arisen because, as seems to be the case with the other philosophical problems of psychology, the problem of laws and principles is not to be solved experimentally but by convention, and so far no conventions have been adopted. They have not been adopted except on a kind of pragmatic basis, which appears to be true for the other philosophical problems as well. Stated differently, the problem of what laws and principles are, really, cannot be solved with an experiment because, like the problem of metaphysics, it is not a question of fact but a question about the basic nature of reality, and no matter how we try, we will probably never know reality without assuming something about it (whatever it may be).

Consequently, it would appear that the problem of laws and principles as well as many other philosophical problems of psychology will be solved, if at all, by convention or consensus, and the current consensus in psychology seems to be that laws are either functional or correlational relationships between either independent and dependent or several dependent variables, respectively. By contrast, principles are more general, or abstract, statements made about, or based on, such laws.

9

The Problem of Anthropomorphism

The magnitude of this problem is not necessarily directly proportional to the length of the word used to identify it. To anthropomorphize is to "humanize the brute," and it has a counterpart for nonhumans called zoomorphism, which is, very loosely, to "brutalize the human." Anthropomorphism is the perhaps unwarranted assignment of human characteristics to animals when there is insufficient, if any, evidence for doing so. It apparently is so pervasive that Hediger (1968, p. 84) asserted "the history of behaviour study is at bottom the history of the struggle against the deeply seated tendency in every human being to humanize the animal."

The problem appears to have been first clearly focused for comparative psychologists by George John Romanes (ca. 1882) when he argued that:

Just as the theologians tell us—and logically enough—that if there is a Divine Mind, the best, and indeed only, conception we can form of it is that which is formed on the analogy, however imperfect, supplied by the human mind; so with 'inverted anthropomorphism' we must apply a similar consideration with a similar conclusion to the animal mind. The mental states of an insect may be widely different from those of a man, and yet most probably the nearest conception that we can form of their true nature is that which we form by assimilating them to the pattern of the only mental states with which we are actually acquainted. And this consideration, it is needless to point out, has a special validity to the evolutionist, inasmuch as upon his theory there must be a psychological, no less than a physiological, continuity extending throughout the length and breadth of the animal kingdom. [Romanes, 1965, p. 461]

Romanes developed and used what has since come to be known as the anecdotal method in his investigations. The method involved the selective accumulation of both popular and scientific stories about the behavior of animals. They were selected according to certain rules for evidence of mental characteristics, and, interestingly, the major rule was whether a living organism was able to learn from its own individual experience; if it could, there was evidence for mind. The most significant limitation of the method was, and still is, that the validity of the stories could not be assessed, and consequently "the tendency to anthropomorphize—to read human motives and abilities into animal behavior—played into Romanes' hands, since he wished to demonstrate a continuity between man and animal. . ." (Marx and Hillix, 1963, p. 132).

As is well known, the suggestion of a continuity between man and animals for both physiological and psychological characteristics had appeared earlier in the work of Charles Darwin (ca. 1859) who, in his later work *The Expression of the Emotions in Man and Animals* (1873), also appeared to indulge in the practice of anthropomorphism. For example, he observed that:

> Action of all kinds, if regularly accompanying any state of the mind, are at once recognized as expressive. These may consist of movements of any part of the body, as the wagging of a dog's tail, the shrugging of a man's shoulders, the erection of the hair, the exudation of perspiration, the state of the capillary circulation, laboured breathing, and the use of the vocal or other sound-producing instruments. Even insects express anger, terror, jealousy, and love by their stridulation. . . . [Darwin, 1968, p. 184]

A relatively short time later, Conwy Lloyd Morgan (ca. 1894) began to battle the practice with his canon sometimes compared to William of Occam's Razor and also referred to, on occasion, as the law of parsimony. Lloyd Morgan's canon advises students of animal behavior that "*in no case may we interpret an action as the outcome of the exercise of a higher psychical faculty, if it can be interpreted as the outcome of the exercise of one which stands lower in the psychological scale*" (in Herrnstein and Boring, 1965, p. 464). Herrnstein and Boring (1965, p. 462) remarked that "with this injunction, he was trying to restrain the undisciplined anthropomorphism — really anthropopsychism — of some of his fellow Darwinians."

Despite such efforts, the practice apparently has persisted into the present. For example, Ivan P. Pavlov (1966, p. 426) noted that

> Were the investigator to speak of the psychical faculties of the higher animals, he would be transferring ideas from his own inner world to nature, repeating the procedures of his predecessors who were accustomed, on observing nature, to apply to its inanimate phenomena their own thoughts, wishes, and sensations.

Similarly, Hull (1943, p. 24) recognized its limitations for experimental work and especially theory construction in his remark that:

> This surreptitious substitution and acceptance of one's knowledge of what needs to be done in a biological emergency for a theoretical deduction is the essence of what we shall call *anthropomorphism,* or the *subjective,* in behavior theory. After many centuries the physical sciences have largely banished the subjective from their fields, but for various reasons this is far less easy of accomplishment and is far less well advanced in the field of behavior. The only known cure for this unfortunate tendency to which all men are more or less subject is a grim and inflexible insistence that all deductions take place according to the explicitly formulated rules stating the functional relationships of A to X and of X to B. This latter is the

essence of the scientifically *objective*. A genuinely scientific theory no more needs the anthropomorphic intuitions of the theorist to eke out the deduction of its implications than an automatic calculating machine needs the intuitions of the operator in the determination of a quotient, once the keys representing the dividend and the divisor have been depressed.

More will be said about objectivity later. For now, it is sufficient to note that Hull equated anthropomorphism with subjectivity.

A few pages later, he suggested several prophylaxes against the practice and then noted that

one of the greatest obstacles to the attainment of a genuine theory of behavior is anthropomorphic subjectivism. At bottom this is because we ourselves are so intimately involved in the problem; we are so close to it that it is difficult to attain adequate perspective. For the reader who has not hitherto struggled with the complex but fascinating problems of behavior theory, it will be hard to realize the difficulty of maintaining a consistently objective point of view. Even when fully aware of the nature of anthropomorphic subjectivism and its dangers, the most careful and experienced thinker is likely to find himself a victim to its seductions. Indeed, despite the most conscientious effort to avoid this it is altogether probable that there may be found in various parts of the present work hidden elements of the anthropomorphically subjective. [Hull, 1943, p. 27]

In a somewhat different context, Skinner (1969, p. 237) has had occasion to consider the pervasiveness of the problem but did not refer to it as anthropomorphism.

In a demonstration experiment, a hungry pigeon was conditioned to turn around in a clockwise direction. A final, smoothly executed pattern of behavior was shaped by reinforcing successive approximations with food. Students who had watched the demonstration were asked to write an account of what they had seen. Their responses included the following: (1) the pigeon was conditioned to *expect* reinforcement for the right kind of behavior; (2) the pigeon walked around, *hoping* that something would bring the food back again; (3) the pigeon *observed* that a certain behavior seemed to produce a particular result; (4) the pigeon *felt* that food would be given it because of its action; and (5) the pigeon came to *associate* his action with the click of the food-dispenser. The observed facts could be stated respectively as follows: (1) the pigeon was reinforced *when* it emitted a given kind of behavior; (2) the pigeon walked around *until* the food container again appeared; (3) a certain behavior *produced* a particular result; (4) food was given to the pigeon *when* it acted in a given way; and (5) the click of the food-dispenser *was temporally related* to the pigeon's action. These statements describe the contingencies of reinforcement. The expressions "expect," "hope," "observe," "feel," and "associate" go beyond them to identify effects on the pigeon. The effect actually observed was clear enough; the pigeon turned more skillfully and more frequently; but that was not the effect reported by the students. (If pressed, they would doubtless have said that the pigeon turned more skillfully and more frequently *because* it expected, hoped, and felt that if it did so food would appear).

The events reported by the students were observed, if at all, in their own behavior. They were describing what they would have expected, felt, and hoped for under similar circumstances. . . .

It seems clear from these remarks that the character of the problem may have changed somewhat over the years. What began as the problem of assigning human mental characteristics to animals has become more recently the problem of assigning human behavioral characteristics to animals. Whatever form it takes, there is nevertheless abundant evidence that it continues to occur. As recently as 1970, in a collection of essays devoted to the memory of T.C. Schneirla, several authors made particular reference to it and its consequences (cf. Aronson, et. al., 1970).

Perhaps enough instances have been cited to support the contention that it has been, and continues to be, a problem for the science and profession of psychology. Those who have considered it most recently appear unanimous in support of the admonition "Don't do it!" As might be expected, however, their arguments against the practice are not entirely uniform. Some simply say it is an error; others refer to it as a fallacy. It may well be that the rationale Lloyd Morgan developed for his canon, in somewhat modified form, is still appropriate today. Anthropomorphism may unnecessarily overcomplicate what otherwise might be explained more simply. In other words, "Don't do it! It isn't parsimonious."

What appears to be an equally valid reason for not engaging in the practice is that it apparently is not possible to know whether, in fact, animals have human characteristics or, indeed, whether humans have animal characteristics, since in either case, they are probably human constructions developed by men to order their sense experience as suggested earlier in connection with the problems of metaphysics and reification. There appears to be as much justification for supposing that animals and men have the same characteristics as for supposing that they do not, but it cannot be known whether they, in fact, have them, just as it is not possible to know whether two humans have the same characteristics; the issue would seem to be what characteristics to assign to either animals or men.

For example, Waters (1948) referred to another practice related to that of anthropomorphism which he called mechanomorphism. It is "the ascription of mechanical characteristics to the human individual, and the interpretation of human behavior in terms of concepts and processes characteristic of machines" (p. 139). Those who engage in this practice might be thought of as anti-anthropomorphists, and they apparently

have embraced only physico-chemical principles of explanations for both human and animal behavior. They have somewhat cavalierly relegated all other explanations to the ash pile of outmoded, anthropomorphic and mentalistic hypotheses of an antiquated medievalism. [Waters, 1948, p. 139]

Since anthropomorphism may unnecessarily overcomplicate explanations of behavior, and since mechanomorphism may unnecessarily oversimplify them, perhaps an entirely different approach to the explanation of behavior is in order. It was discussed earlier as a form of empirical explanation and requires neither the assignment of human characteristics to animals nor the ascription of mechanical characteristics to humans. It is, rather, a form of explanation based on the variables of which behavior is a function, that is, its laws, and was referred to earlier as a functional explanation.

It might be argued, with some justification, that men can do nothing but anthropomorphize. All knowledge is human knowledge and is expressed in human form; hence, it is anthropomorphic. The argument is probably valid but is based on a somewhat different meaning for the term than is usually intended within psychology. In psychology, anthropomorphism refers to a particular practice, like reification, that apparently can be avoided. In the above argument, the term refers to nearly everything that man does, especially in his efforts to know. Consequently, while the argument cannot be refuted, it can be ignored; since that meaning is so ubiquitous, it allows for no distinctions. In general, those psychologists, or behavioral scientists, who have devoted much thought to the problem might agree that the slogan "Eschew Anthropomorphism" above the portals of every behavioral laboratory would help to remind those who pass through them of this philosophical problem of psychology; it is not likely to be solved in any other way.

101

10

The Problem of Purpose

The problem of purpose is whether it occurs in, is observed in, or is imposed on behavior. As might be expected, it arises most frequently within the area of motivation in psychology but is not necessarily restricted to it. For example, in his book *Milestones in Motivation*, Russell (1970, p. 148) remarked:

> No one doubts that some, if not all, behavior can be most efficiently described by reference to the end toward which it is directed. Purposeful behavior is seen as characteristic of man and is often imputed to other species as well. Psychologists have most typically divided into two camps on the subject of purpose. On the one hand, there are those, like many instinct theorists, who assume purpose to be so intrinsic to all behavior that it

must be accepted as a given, a postulate which in itself demands no explanation. On the other hand, there are those, like the drive theorists, who doubt that purpose can be dealt with in scientific terms at all. They tend to deny that behavior may be purposeful and to see apparent examples of purposiveness as mere artifacts of blind adaptive mechanisms. A generation of psychologists, imbued with the spirit of drive theory, seemed to repress the very problem of direction in behavior, not only in their claim that activation was the sole function of motivation but in their refusal to deal with the issue seriously under any other heading. Many were not aware that purpose had ever been a problem for psychologists.

In this selection, the author not only acknowledges that purpose has been a problem for psychologists, but he also recognizes that purpose is "often imputed to other species." If purposeful behavior is a "characteristic of man," the imputation of purpose to other species is an instance of anthropomorphism and lends further support to the proposition that anthropomorphism is a persistent and pervasive philosophical problem of psychology.

Immediately following the above statement, Russell cited developments in engineering, cybernetics, and computer technology which suggest that, since mechanical and electronic devices can be constructed in such a way that they behave as though they were purposeful, it apparently exists in behavior and can be the subject of empirical inquiry. However, such developments do not so much prove the existence of purpose as they beg the question of purpose, since the mechanical and electronic devices were constructed, by humans, so that they exhibited those types of behavior that, in humans, would be called purposeful. Hence, a third camp of those who divide on the subject of purpose might consist of those who doubt that purpose refers to a class of events to be explained in psychology. Nevertheless, there is no doubt that purpose is a rich tradition in psychology. Indeed, it could well be that the problem of purpose, and efforts to resolve it, account in very large part for the emergence of psychology as a natural science.

At some point in nearly every discussion of purpose, some reference is made to teleology. Skinner (1969, p. 105) has called it a "specter," and so now may be as good a time as any to see whether it is possible to "lay the ghost." Briefly, teleology may be formally defined as the study of ends or final causes. For psychologists, the doctrine of teleology is that present events are determined by their consequences, final effects, or future events. If they are, then the teleological problem is how events that have not yet occurred, future events, could possibly serve as determinants for, or in any way influence, those events that are now occurring, present events; the problem is how the future can affect the present when the future has not yet occurred. Both Hull and Skinner have considered this aspect of the problem of purpose in somewhat different ways.

For example, Hull (1943, p. 26) stated:

Perhaps the very natural and economical mode of communication whereby we speak of the terminal or goal phases of action, largely regardless of the antecedent movements involved, predisposes us to a belief in *teleology*. In its extreme form teleology is the name of the belief that the *terminal* stage of certain environmental-organismic interaction cycles somehow is at the same time one of the *antecedent* determining conditions which bring the behavior cycle about. This approach, in the case of a purposive behavior situation not hitherto known to the theorist, involves a kind of logical circularity: to deduce the outcome of any behavioral situation in the sense of the deductive predictions here under consideration, it is necessary to know all the relevant antecedent conditions, but these cannot be determined until the behavioral outcome has been deduced. In effect this means that the task of deduction cannot begin until after it is completed! Naturally this leaves the theorist completely helpless. It is not surprising that the doctrine of teleology leads to theoretical despair and to such pseudo-remedies as vitalism and *emergentism*.

Emergentism, as applied to organismic behavior, is the name for the view that in the process of evolution there has "emerged" a form of behavior which is ultimately unanalyzable into logically more primitive elements—behavior which cannot possibly be deduced from any logically prior principles whatever. In particular it is held that what is called goal or purposive behavior is of such a nature, that it cannot be derived from any conceivable set of postulates involving mere stimuli and mere movement.

His view was that derivations of that sort could, in fact, be made from such postulates, and so he accepted goal, or purposive, behaviors as events to be explained by his theory.

On the other hand, Skinner (1969, pp. 105-9) remarked that:

> We are interested in the behavior of an organism because of its effects on the environment. (One effect on the social environment is, of course, the arousal of our interest.) Some effects seem to throw light on the behavior which produces them, but their explanatory role has been clouded by the fact that they follow the behavior and therefore raise the specter of teleology.
>
> An attempt has been made to solve the problem by creating a prior surrogate of a given effect. A quality or property of purpose is assigned to behavior to bring "what the organism is behaving for" into the effective present; or the organism is said to behave in a given way because it intends to achieve, or expects to have, a given effect; or its behavior is characterized as possessing utility to the extent that it maximizes or minimizes certain effects. The teleological problem is, of course, not solved until we have answered certain questions: what gives an action its purpose, what leads an organism to expect to have an effect, how is utility represented in behavior?
>
> The answers to such questions are eventually to be found in past instances in which similar behavior has been effective. The original problem can be solved directly in the same way. Thorndike's Law of Effect was a step in that direction; the approximately simultaneous occurrence of a response and

certain environmental events (usually generated by it) changes the responding organism, increasing the probability that responses of the same sort will occur again. The response itself has passed into history and is not altered. By emphasizing a change in the organism, Thorndike's principle made it possible to include the effects of action among the causes of future action without using concepts like purpose, intention, expectancy, or utility. Up to that time, the only demonstrable causes of behavior had been antecedent stimuli. The range of the eliciting stimulus was later to be extended by Pavlovian conditioning, and the concept could be broadened to include the releasers of the ethologists, but only a small part of behavior can be predicted or controlled simply by identifying or manipulating stimuli. The Law of Effect added an important new class of variables of which behavior could be shown to be a function.

Skinner then reviewed some of the recent history of the concept of purpose within psychology and concluded several pages later that:

The contingencies of reinforcement which define operant behavior are widespread if not ubiquitous. Those who are sensitive to this fact are sometimes embarrassed by the frequency with which they see reinforcement everywhere, as Marxists see class struggle or Freudians the Oedipus relation. Yet the fact is that reinforcement is extraordinarily important. That is why it is reassuring to recall that its place was once taken by the concept of purpose; no one is likely to object to a search for purpose in every human act. The difference is that we are now in a position to search effectively. [Skinner, 1969, p. 125]

Thus, for him, the concept of purpose in psychology has been replaced with the concept of reinforcement. Where psychologists formerly attempted to determine the purposes of behavior, they now attempt to determine the reinforcers of behavior or, perhaps more accurately, the variables of which behaviors are a function. The chief difference between the two approaches is that the search for reinforcers can now proceed by way of the technology that has emerged from the experimental analysis of behavior; it was not available to those who sought for purposes.

To return to the teleological problem, Skinner noted that it has been resolved in the past by "creating a prior surrogate of a given effect" such as a purpose, intention, or expectation to bring the future "into the effective present." He would solve it in a somewhat different way. For him, it is not the future consequences of behavior but the past consequences of similar behavior that determine what the organism is presently doing; it is not the future but the past that determines the present. Hence, his solution, if it can be called that, is to eliminate the teleological problem.

However, while his proposal does appear to eliminate it, an equally pressing problem might still be said to remain. That problem has to do with the question of how events that have already occurred could possibly influence, or determine, events that are now occurring; this problem is how the past can affect the present when the past has already occurred. His solution to it is simply to say that the organism has been changed by the past consequences of its behavior. For some, that statement may solve the problem but, in turn, define another and so on, ad infinitum. Such considerations support the selection of purpose as a philosophical problem of psychology, especially since a number of equally philosophical problems are related to it; the specter of teleology may still be among them.

Many other psychologists have published their views on the topic of purpose, although they did not necessarily regard it as a philosophical problem of psychology. Some of them might be described as classical purposivists in the sense that the concept was of central importance to their positions. Two psychologists who can be placed in this group are William McDougall (ca. 1923) and Edward Chace Tolman (ca. 1932). McDougall (cf. Herrnstein and Boring, 1965, pp. 616-18) listed seven characteristics, or marks, of behavior, the last of which was purpose.

> In purposive action . . . the whole organism is commonly involved; the processes of all its parts are subordinated and adjusted in such a way as to promote the better pursuit of the natural goal of the action. If, while you amuse yourself by repeatedly exciting the scratch-reflex in your dog, some sound excites him to behavior, then, even though the behavior consists in nothing more than assuming an alert attitude with eyes and ears directed toward the disturbing object, your stimulation of his flank becomes ineffective. . . . If the sound is followed by the appearance of a stranger

(dog or man) your dog springs to his feet with every muscle and organ at work in preparation for attack. . . . That is the type of the total reaction.

He appears to have viewed purpose as the coordination that could be observed in the actions of an animal with reference to some goal; the concept of goal is of major significance in most discussions of purpose.

For Tolman (1967, pp. 12-13), it apparently was quite obvious that:

Behavior as behavior, that is, as molar, *is* purposive and is cognitive. These purposes and cognitions are of its immediate descriptive warp and woof. It, no doubt, is strictly and completely dependent upon an underlying manifold of physics and chemistry, but initially and as a matter of first identification, behavior as behavior reeks of purpose and of cognition. And such purposes and such cognitions are just as evident, as we shall see later, if this behavior be that of a rat as if it be that of a human being.

Finally, however, it must nonetheless be emphasized that purposes and cognitions which are thus immediately, immanently, in behavior are wholly objective as to definition. They are defined by characters and relationships which we observe out there in the behavior. We, the observers, watch the behavior of the rat, the cat, or the man, and note its character as a getting to such and such by means of such and such a selected pattern of commerces-with. It is we, the independent and neutral observers, who note these perfectly objective characters as immanent in the behavior and have happened to choose the terms *purpose* and *cognition* as generic names for such characters.

Subsequently, and after consideration of Thorndike's description for a cat getting out of a puzzle box, Tolman (1967, p. 14) offered a definition for purpose.

We note two significant features in this description: (a) the fact of the behaving organism's readiness to persist through trial and error, and (b) the fact of his tendency on successive occasions to select sooner and sooner the act which gets him out easily and quickly—i.e., the fact of *docility*. And it is these two correlative features which, we shall now declare, define the immediate character which we call the cat's purpose to get to the freedom outside. The doctrine we here contend for is, in short, that wherever a response shows docility relative to some end—wherever a response is ready (a) to break out into trial and error and (b) to select gradually, or suddenly the more efficient of such trials and errors with respect to getting to that end—such a response expresses and defines something which, for convenience, we name as a purpose. Wherever such a set of facts appears (and where save in the simplest and most rigid tropisms and reflexes does it not?), there we have objectively manifested and defined that which is conveniently called a purpose.

Thus, persistence and docility, or teachableness, are what define purpose for Tolman. Some of his later remarks suggest that he means more than that when he uses the term, but if that is all that is meant, then perhaps it is persistence and docility, rather than purpose, that are of major interest to him; the use of the term *purpose* is perhaps superfluous if not irrelevant.

Somewhat later, purpose was translated into goal-directed behavior as illustrated by Bindra (1959, p. 17) in his systematic reinterpretation of motivation.

If one observes the behavior of an animal in its familiar surroundings, one is likely to be struck by the effectiveness with which it manipulates and adapts to its environment. It feeds, protects, and amuses itself in what appears to be a fairly efficient way. Each response systematically follows, or is accompanied by, others in such a way that the animal usually manages to effect an adaptation in relation to changing objects, events, and other classes of sensory stimulation. The activities of animals seem almost always to be aimed at some particular consequences, directed toward some "goals." In common-sense language we say that behavior tends to be "purposive" or that animals "have purposes." It is this "purposive" or "moving-in-the-direction-of-goals" aspect of behavior that is the dominant feature of the phenomena that are termed motivational, and that has been generally considered to present the core of the psychological problem of motivation.

For Bindra (1959, p. 18), the current consensus is "that the core of what is usually called the problem of motivation lies in the 'purposive' or goal-directed aspect of behavior. This feature is also to be found in perceptual and other 'nonmotivational' activities, but it is particularly evident in motivational phenomena."

He subsequently observed that:

> Common sense considers "purpose" to be an entirely subjective concept. For the layman, purpose is synonymous with an experience of intention or a preconceived plan to do something. If purpose is to be defined only in this subjective sense, the scientist cannot give it objective meaning or study it. For us purpose must somehow refer to certain objectively observable aspects of behavior. To avoid confusion, psychologists have adopted the term *goal direction* to refer to the purposive aspect of observed behavior, leaving the term *purpose* for the common-sense subjective connotations of intention or consciousness of some aim. [Bindra, 1959, pp. 51-52]

Common sense and the layman may have been somewhat mistreated in these passages, but they do serve to illustrate that Bindra, as did Tolman, accepted as given "certain objectively observable aspects of behavior" as though they occur, and can be observed, in behavior. The one selected was the purposive aspect, which was then equated with goal direction. If purposive behavior is to be equated with goal-directed behavior, the question of what constitutes a goal then arises. In answer to this question, Bindra (1959, pp. 54-55) stated that

> what we ordinarily call a goal is something more than an incentive; a goal is a special class of

incentive. An incentive becomes a goal when it is treated as a goal; that is, when it is selected, arbitrarily, as the focus or "anchor" with respect to which the behavior of the organism is described. A moment's reflection will show that whether an object (e.g. food) is described as an incentive or as a goal depends only on whether the investigator has selected it as the reference point for the description of behavior. Thus, when we say, for example, that food is the goal for a hungry animal, we are asserting that (1) we know that food is an incentive for the animal, and (2) *we* have chosen to describe the behavior of the animal in relation to food rather than with reference to any other object or event. A *goal* is thus *an incentive that is chosen by the investigator as a reference point for describing observed behavior.*

The choice of the reference point—called goal—is completely arbitrary and has reference only to the investigator's mode of analysis, not to the animal's intention or any other subjective state. Of course, on the basis of his past experience, an investigator normally knows what objects and events are likely to serve as incentives under what conditions, and his choice of a particular object as the goal is determined by this knowledge. Thus, when the animal is known to be hungry, the investigator usually considers food as the goal; when the animal is on an electrified grid, the investigator considers termination of the electric current as the goal. However, the fact that whether an object or event does serve as an incentive depends upon the animal's makeup and its momentary state does not alter the basic fact that a goal is an incentive that the investigator chooses to consider as the reference point for the description of behavior.

If goals are arbitrarily selected by an investigator as a "reference point for the description of behavior," it would seem that the language of purpose and goals is itself somewhat arbitrary. In other words, whether behavior is described with reference to purposes, or goals, or something else depends upon the predilections of the investigator. He might find that behavior can be described without them, and, since it has, there is at least some doubt that purpose either occurs or is observed in behavior; it more likely is imposed on behavior. For that matter, there is some doubt that purpose is in any way required for an adequate account of behavior. One consequence of such considerations is that the problem of purpose almost disappears; perhaps that is the only way it can be solved.

11

The Problem of Freedom

As with many of the other philosophical
problems of psychology, psychologists seem
compelled to resurrect this one from time to time if only
to see whether there is anything new about it in the light
of current developments. A historian of psychology has
remarked recently that "despite the antiquity of the
problem and despite its metaphysical overtones, it
continues to be a challenge to every generation of
psychologists" (Klein, 1970, p. 314); the present one
apparently is no exception to that rule. In addition, for
many, and especially beginning, students of psychology, as well as for many informed laymen who become
interested in psychology, it is one of those problems
that psychology is all about; for them, it is one of those
problems that define psychology, although most psychologists would reject that view of the discipline.

A rather recent version of this problem with Aristotelian overtones is whether conduct, or behavior, occurs by chance or whether it is determined. If it occurs by chance, choice apparently is possible, and consequently men, in particular, can be held responsible as well as praised or blamed for what they do. If it is determined, choice apparently is not possible, and hence responsibility, praise, and blame are irrelevant to what men do. If responsibility, praise, and blame are irrelevant to what they do, then there appears to be no basis for evaluating human worth or dignity (cf. Skinner, 1971, pp. 19-22).

The problem has not always been stated in quite that form and, since William James is still considered by some to be the greatest American psychologist, an examination of his statement of it does not appear out of order. In his chapter on "Will," which he equated with the effort or power of thought, James (1950, p. 571) remarked that:

It certainly appears to us indeterminate, and as if, even with an unchanging object, we might make more or less, as we choose. If it be really indeterminate, our future acts are ambiguous or unpredestinate; in common parlance, *our wills are free*. If the amount of effort be not indeterminate, but be related in a fixed manner to the objects themselves, in such wise that whatever object at any time fills our consciousness was from eternity bound to fill it then and there, and compel from us the exact effort, neither more nor less, which we bestow upon it,—then our wills are not free, and all our acts are foreordained. *The question of fact in the free-will controversy is thus extremely simple.* It relates solely to the amount of effort of attention or consent which we can at any time put forth. Are the duration and intensity of this effort fixed functions of the object, or are they not?

James (1950, p. 573) resolved the problem in favor of freedom on an "ethical rather than psychological" basis. However, what is important about his remarks for this discussion is not his solution but his formulation of the problem. For him, the problem was whether the power or effort of thought is free, whereas in the more recent version presented earlier, the problem was whether behavior is free; for many, the recent version may appear the more likely to be solved with the methods of science.

A rather different perspective on this problem was expressed by Edwin G. Boring (1957*b*, p. 190) by way of an anecdote about one of his exchanges with William McDougall.

Years ago William McDougall, the psychologist, was my colleague at Harvard. He believed in freedom for the human mind—in at least a little residue of freedom—believed in it and hoped for as much as he could save from the inroads of scientific determinism. To the determinist-psychologists, such a view was scientifically immoral. John B. Watson, behaviorism's founder, reviewed McDougall's textbook of 1923 under the title "Professor McDougall returns to religion," and you may be sure that Watson was not thinking of himself as a rejoicing father welcoming back a prodigal. I used to wonder about McDougall and determinism, and then one afternoon in a colloquium—one of those rare occasions when argument brings insight and does not merely serve to harden preconceptions—I found out where lay the difference between us—McDougall, the voluntarist, and me, the determinist. McDougall's freedom was my variance. McDougall hoped that variance would always be found in specifying the laws of behavior, for there freedom might still persist. I hoped then—less wise than I think I am now . . .—that science would keep pressing variance toward zero as a limit. At any rate this general fact emerges from this example: freedom, when you believe it is operating, always resides in an area of ignorance. If there is a known law, you do not have freedom.

Later in that same article, he remarked that "freedom is a negative conception. It is the absence of causes," and "men will hypostatize a negative into a positive, as they have done with the concept of freedom and also with the concept of chance. Both *freedom* and *chance* are terms that are used when efficient causes of present events are not known and often appear to be unknowable" (Boring, 1957*b*, p. 192).

Herbert Feigl (1959, p. 116) formulated the problem of freedom in a somewhat different way in his discussion of some philosophical embarrassments of psychology. During that discussion and in what appears to have been a fit of good humor, he referred to philosophy "as the disease of which it should be the cure"; there are those who might say the same of psychology. The significance of his formulation of, and apparent solution to, the problem of freedom for the present discussion is that he, along with others, recognizes that human freedom of choice or action is not guaranteed by the physical principle of indeterminacy.

An early interpretation of this principle has been rather clearly expressed for a lay audience that includes psychologists by Ludwig Immergluck (1964, p. 272) who revisited the ancient problem of determinism-freedom in contemporary psychology during the last decade. Essentially, this interpretation states that either the position or the velocity of a particle can be known with some accuracy, but both cannot be known at the same time because the process of observation interferes with one when the other is being measured.

A more recent version of this principle is that neither the position nor the velocity of a particle can be known with accuracy. Rather, both can be known only as two different frequency distributions of measurements. Whatever the interpretation, the principle does not demonstrate that absolute chance is a positive factor operating in the universe except in relation to our systems of concepts about the universe; indeed, there does not appear to be any way in which such a demonstration could be accomplished. Hence, the principle still cannot be used to prove the existence of human freedom.

In an earlier section of his article, Immergluck (1964, p. 271) remarked that

> any attempts to mold both determinism and free will into some kind of unitary conceptual schema may likely serve to benefit only the free-will half of the dichotomy, and might in effect constitute a philosophic recommitment to psychological vitalism. It takes but one honest-to-goodness spook to prove the existence of ghosts, only one unnatural

event to establish the existence of a supernature, and only one free-will act to contradict determinism.

What he may have overlooked is that the methods of science, as they are currently understood at least, cannot tell us what is a "free-will act."

As mentioned earlier in relation to the problem of theory, the methods of science are basically observational; they are based on observations made somewhere, sometime, by someone under controlled conditions. In principle, at least, observations are infinite in number; the someone making them could go on doing so forever provided he could muster the requisite immortality. Since he cannot, the immortality is achieved by those who develop a similar interest and continue where he must stop.

However, the observations of those who follow are also infinite since, after the last observation has been made, another one always can be made. Consequently, and in a sense regardless of indeterminacy, it is for this reason, as well as the fact that scientists do not just observe but also draw conclusions based on their observations, that science eventually resorts to some form of statistical analysis, specifically inferential statistics, to help resolve the dilemma.

Inferential statistics at some critical point always compares an obtained result, based on observation, to those results that would be expected by chance, or, to the results that would be expected if all effects were random or chance effects. The hypothesis that is tested is referred to as the null hypothesis. It is a statement of what would be expected by chance, and the statistical test is formulated expressly for the purpose of allowing the investigator or scientist to reject it. If he can reject the null hypothesis, he then can say that the effects he observed had a certain rather low probability of having occurred by chance. If he cannot reject it, or must accept it, no such statement can be made, and he must conclude that the effects he observed were no different than those he would expect by chance. However, by doing so, he has not proved that only chance factors are operating; he has only shown that the effects he observed did not differ from those to be expected by chance. No amount of scientific investigation will ever prove that only chance factors are operating. The methods of science beg the question of chance; they assume it and, hence, cannot be used to prove it. Such a statement is simply another way of saying that the methods of science cannot prove the null hypothesis; they can only disprove it. This point, or one very similar to it, has been made in a somewhat different context by Frank Beach (1955) with regard to the descent of instinct.

A "free-will act" would require that the null hypothesis be proved. That is, to say that an act is a "free-will act" is to say that it is not predictable or related to any antecedent or preceding condition or, for that matter, to any other set of events or conditions. That statement would require that experiments be designed not to demonstrate an effect rather than to demonstrate one, and that procedure is simply contrary to the purposes for which experimentation and statistical inference evolved in science. The methods of science are deterministic; they cannot be used to tell us what is a "free-will act," but they can tell us what is not.

One implication of these considerations is that science can tell us what acts are predictable; that is what is meant by the statement that it is positive or positivistic. However, it cannot tell us that all acts are predictable because all acts have not yet been examined nor are they likely to be; it is to be hoped that most of them have not yet occurred. Hence, the question of whether all behavior is determined is an open one; it could well be the case that some behaviors are determined and some are not, but only those that are can be known to be so with present methods. Science, behavioral or otherwise, cannot tell men that they are free to act; it can only tell them that sometimes they are not. It is conceivable that a class of "pure, spontaneous acts" occurs, but it is not likely that any of the members of that class will be known, at least with the methods of science as they are currently understood.

Consequently, all is not well for freedom but neither is it for determinism. Most textbooks devoted to the experimental aspects of psychology list determinism as one of the "necessary presuppositions" of science as though, if the reader did not make that assumption on the spot, he could read no further and so might as well either apply for a refund or burn the book. However, the necessity of presuppositions appears to be a logical rather than an empirical matter. It is possible that someone might enter the behavioral laboratory and observe some behavior under controlled conditions without ever having read, or been told, about the assumptions he must make before he could do so, including the assumption of order. If order emerged from his observations, he might report it, but he would not necessarily have to assume it was there before he started observing. The universe does not, because of logical necessity, have to be either ordered or determined for there to be any science.

It may well be that, in many or most instances, the methods of science are used without presuppositions but with apparent presuppositions imposed after the fact of their use on the basis of logical necessity. In addition, if order emerges from their application, it does not necessarily have to be there before they were applied, except perhaps for a logician who is also a metaphysical realist. The "presuppositions of science" seem to be based on a logical analysis of what science is all about, but they may be totally at variance with how science, in fact, is conducted if that could ever be known. In other words, there may be some behavioral scientists who are neither voluntarists nor determinists. If such a statement seems logically absurd, it is only because of the assumption that, if they are not one, they are the other, as in the case of freedom versus determinism.

Carl R. Rogers, a psychologist of a somewhat different persuasion than B.F. Skinner, debated with him the issue of freedom and the control of men; the present discussion is relevant to that debate but does not necessarily resolve their differences. Professor Skinner (1961, pp. 7-8) held that:

So long as the findings and methods of science are applied to human affairs only in a sort of remedial patchwork, we may continue to hold any view of human nature we like. But as the use of science increases, we are forced to accept the theoretical structure with which science represents its facts. The difficulty is that this structure is clearly at odds with the traditional democratic conception of man. Every discovery of an event which has a part in shaping a man's behavior seems to leave so much the less to be credited to the man himself; and as such explanations become more and more comprehensive, the contribution which may be claimed by the individual himself appears to approach zero. Man's vaunted creative powers, his original accomplishments in art, science, and morals, his capacity to choose and our right to hold him responsible for the consequences of his choice—none of these is conspicuous in this new self-portrait. Man, we once believed, was free to express himself in art, music, and literature, to inquire into nature, to seek salvation in his own way. He could initiate action and make spontaneous and capricious changes of course. Under the most extreme duress some sort of choice remained to him. He could resist any effort to control him, though it might cost him his life. But science insists that action is initiated by forces impinging upon the individual, and that caprice is only another name for behavior for which we have not yet found a cause.

Professor Rogers (Rogers and Skinner, 1956, p. 1064) claimed he understood that point of view but believed that

it avoids looking at the great paradox of behavioral science. Behavior, when it is examined scientifically, is surely best understood as determined by prior causation. This is one great fact of science. But responsible personal choice, which is the most essential element in being a person, which is the core experience in psychotherapy, which exists prior to any scientific endeavor, is an equally prominent fact in our lives. To deny the experience of responsible choice is, to me, as restricted a view as to deny the possibility of a behavioral science.

This debate was of some significance for perhaps clarifying their positions, although there are those who might protest that it generated more heat than light. Nevertheless, there are at least two items that emerged from it of somewhat major importance for this discussion of the problem of freedom. The first is that science has shown there are a good many instances in which men are not free, and there are probably a great many more yet to be demonstrated. However, they have not yet been demonstrated, and until they are, the assumption that all behavioral events are determined remains an assumption. Indeed, it probably will always remain an assumption because of the limitations of science examined earlier in this discussion. Consequently, if we "accept the theoretical structure with which science represents its facts," it is accepted not necessarily because it is true but perhaps simply because it is more useful than any other structure that has so far evolved. We are not forced to accept it because of its unquestioned veracity but because of its utility, and the utility of a conceptual structure is not indefinite nor is the structure necessarily unique.

The second item of importance for this discussion of freedom is that the experience of freedom may in fact occur, but it is no guarantee that men are therefore free. The experience of freedom does not prove the existence of freedom any more than the feeling that knowledge is certain proves the existence of certain knowledge. The experience of freedom may be intuitively true in the sense that it is known directly, but it is not proof for the existence of freedom since, if experiences are behavioral events and at least some behavioral events are determined, the experience of freedom may not have been determined by freedom as a positive factor operating in the universe but, rather, may have been shaped up by the literature of freedom so frequently referred to by Professor Skinner. The facts of experience are not necessarily indubitable proof for the existence of whatever it is they are about. Men may proclaim their freedom when, in fact, they are in bondage to the literature of freedom, and the problem of freedom for a science of behavior is that it cannot be known whether there are any instances in which men are free, although there appear to be a great many in which they are not.

12

The Problem of
Knowledge

For most people, this problem has to do with how something that is "out there" in the environment gets "in here" inside the head, as though there were something that is transmitted, transferred, or transported in the process of knowing. "By the ancients, and by unreflecting people perhaps today, knowledge is explained as the passage of something from without into the mind—the latter, so far, at least, as its sensible affections go, being passive and receptive" (James, 1950, p. 219).

For William James (1950, p. 216), knowing appears to have been a basic fact of experience that required no further explanation and perhaps could not be given one.

> Now the *relation of knowing* is the most mysterious thing in the world. If we ask how one thing

can know another we are led into the heart of *Erkenntnisstheorie* and metaphysics. The psychologist, for his part, does not consider the matter so curiously as this. Finding a world before him which he cannot but believe that *he* knows, and setting himself to study his own past thoughts, or someone else's thoughts, of what he believes to be that same world; he cannot but conclude that those other thoughts know it after their fashion even as he knows it after his. Knowledge becomes for him an ultimate relation that must be admitted, whether it be explained or not, just like difference or resemblance, which no one seeks to explain.

Of course, the problem of knowledge had been raised some time before James wrote about it. For example, in her discussion of prescientific psychology, which covers a period of time from the pre-Socratic philosophers to Wilhelm Wundt, Edna Heidbreder (1933, p. 20) remarked that "in philosophy, psychology is likely to be encountered as epistemology. In their attempts to comprehend the universe, philosophers are sooner or later arrested by the thought 'how can we know?' and this question gives rise to an examination of human ways of knowing. . . ."

The questions "How can we know?" as well as "How do we know?" help to reveal how knowledge can be a problem. The first is related to the validity, or criteria, of knowledge, whereas the second has to do with the process of knowing; the second is considered, by many, to be the traditional problem of knowledge in psychology. An additional question that helps to reveal how knowledge can be a problem is the somewhat paradoxical "How do we know that we know?" To know that we know would seem to require that either or both the criteria of knowledge and the process of knowing be known before we even can begin to know.

The question "How do we know?" not only helps to define knowledge as a problem but appears to require a statement about the means by which we know; in that sense, it is a question of methodology. Furthermore, if that question is inseparable from the question "How can we know?", an answer to the first may also answer the second; it is not entirely clear what can be done about the third except perhaps to ignore it.

For most psychologists, the means by which we know is the methodology of science, although that may not be immediately obvious to students of psychology and those who develop an interest in psychology. Nevertheless, when psychologists are asked how they know something about behavior, for example, they most often refer to data obtained under controlled conditions of observation. Consequently, it would seem that the methodology of psychology is its epistemology, or its theory of knowledge; that is, the epistemology of psychology, as well as the other sciences, is the epistemology of science, and it, in turn, is the methodology of science.

However, despite extensive efforts to state what it is, there does not appear to be any one method that can be referred to as the scientific method; perhaps that circumstance results whenever an attempt is made to state the "essence" of something. Nevertheless, many psychologists have attempted to formulate a view of it. For example, Corso (1967, pp. 7-8) remarked that it consists of five phases. They are: the statement of a problem; the formulation of an hypothesis; the collection of data in a controlled testing situation; the organization and analysis of the data; and finally, the evaluation and generalization of the findings to other problem areas. Similarly, McGuigan (1968, p. 12) stated that the method consists of a series of steps including a statement of the problem, the formulation of an hypothesis, the collection of data, the comparison of the data with the hypothesis, the generalization of the confirmed hypothesis to other situations, and the prediction of results in new situations that have not yet been examined. In all fairness to both authors, it should be recorded that they recognize any statement of what the method is may be quite arbitrary.

On the other hand, in "A Case History in Scientific Method," B.F. Skinner (1961, pp. 78-79) remarked that:

> If we are interested in perpetuating the practices responsible for the present corpus of scientific knowledge, we must keep in mind that some very important parts of the scientific process do not now lend themselves to mathematical, logical, or any other formal treatment. We do not know enough about human behavior to know how the scientist does what he does. Although statisticians and methodologists may seem to tell us, or at least imply, how the mind works—how problems arise, how hypotheses are formed, deductions made, and crucial experiments designed—we as psychologists are in a position to remind them that they do not have methods appropriate to the empirical observation or the functional analysis of such data. These are aspects of human behavior, and no one knows better than we how little can at the moment be said about them.

Despite these considerations, there does appear to be some element of commonality across the various statements on scientific methodology. It is that, at some point, the conjectures or speculations of a scientist are submitted to some sort of empirical test under controlled conditions of observation. Perhaps that is about as much as can be said about the "essence" of scientific methodology or the epistemology of science at the present time.

How psychology came to adopt the epistemology of science has been rather thoroughly documented by R.S. Peters (1965) in his abridged one-volume edition of *Brett's History of Psychology*. As Heidbreder (1933, p. 25) mentioned almost incidentally in an earlier part of her discussion, "very early, philosophers had distinguished between knowledge gained by the senses and knowledge achieved by reason." Peters referred to these two ways of knowing as the observationalist and rationalist traditions, respectively; they are more commonly identified as empiricism and rationalism.

In general, empiricism is the view that all knowledge is obtained by means of the senses, sensation, or sense experience. The method for acquiring knowledge is observation based on the logic of induction and primarily that by simple enumeration; induction is the next philosophical problem of psychology to be examined. By contrast, rationalism is the view that all knowledge is obtained by means of the intellect, reflection, or reason. The method for acquiring knowledge is ratiocination based primarily on the logic of deduction. According to some authors (e.g., Hull, 1943, p. 381), these two views of knowing have been synthesized in most modern conceptions of science; that is, science is commonly said to have both empirical and rational components.

The empirical component of science consists of sense experience, observations, or data obtained inductively under controlled conditions of observation. The rational component of science consists of symbols, or systems of symbols, by means of which sense experience, observations, or data are recorded and then deductively related to one another. The facts, laws, principles, and theories that emerge from the dynamic interplay between these major components of science are what scientists usually mean by scientific knowledge.

Considerations of this kind are what most psychologists have come to identify as philosophy of science. For example, the discussion of scientific methodology by Corso (1967) can be found under that title in the first chapter of his text. In general, philosophy of science is not itself science but is about science. That is, philosophers of science do not do science in the sense that they perform experiments or test hypotheses under controlled conditions. Rather, their major concern is to state what it is that scientists do, although their methods for finding out are primarily analytic, or rational, as opposed to that combination of rationalism and empiricism that is characteristic of the methodology of science.

Since what it is that scientists do is their behavior, and since psychology frequently is described as the science of behavior, it might be expected as suggested in the above remarks by Skinner that psychologists would have more to say on the subject than philosophers and that psychology, in fact, has been somewhat derelict in the omission. This point of view has recently been expressed by Wolman (1971, p. 884). However, his proposal is that psychology develop its own philosophy of science in what appears to be the traditional analytic sense. Another approach may be simply to extend the science of behavior to include the behavior of scientists.

A few psychologists may find it somewhat laughable to say so, but perhaps Professor Skinner was too modest in his assessment of what psychologists know about the behavior of scientists. Whatever else they may do, it seems rather obvious that scientists are engaged in learning, whether it is about the universe or their own sense experience. Perhaps most, if not all, of their behavior can be accounted for as trial and success, rather than trial and error, learning; their errors are not usually recorded nor do they appear to be as effective in altering their behavior as are their successes. Furthermore, since trial and success learning is simply another name for operant conditioning, it may be that nearly all the behavior of scientists can be explained by the principles of operant conditioning that Professor Skinner has helped to formulate.

This apparent digression is relevant to the problem of knowledge in the following way. If behavioral scientists are engaged in the task of learning about behavior, and if some of them are concerned especially with the topic of learning, then some behavioral scientists are learning about learning; paradoxically, they are being operantly conditioned by operant conditioning. Whether paradoxical or not, another implication is that, if to know something means that is has been learned, then it would appear that all that psychologists have learned about learning is what is known about knowing. In other words, the reply to the question "How do we know?" appears to be "We learn" and that is how we know. Interestingly, that reply seems to answer both "How do we know?" as well as "How can we know?" since to know is to be able to know.

This view, or one very much like it, has been expressed by Skinner on a number of occasions in a number of contexts. For example, in *The Technology of Teaching*, he remarked that:

> "To impart knowledge" is *to bring behavior of given topography under the control of given variables.*
>
> A curious feature of knowledge, as traditionally conceived, is that it must be stored. We are said to "memorize" our experiences, a metaphor presumably derived from the practice of making external records for future reference. Committing to memory is regarded as a cognitive act. There is a temporal discrepancy between input and output, and it is therefore supposed that an inner record of input is made and stored and later retrieved and converted into output. The supposition is made plausible by the analogy with computers which do indeed store and retrieve—in a mechanized version of a more primitive use of actual records.
>
> [A few paragraphs later, he observed that] the experimental analysis of behavior has no need for a concept of memory in the sense of a storehouse in which records of variables are kept and later retrieved for use. An organism is changed when exposed to contingencies of reinforcement and survives as a changed organism. It responds in different ways and under different circumstances,

and that is as close as we come to the storage of "knowing how." The storage of "knowing about" seems to raise a special problem, but *the contingencies which have modified an organism are not stored within the organism.* The student who has learned a list of nonsense syllables, like the priest who has learned a Veda, has acquired a special repertoire in which responses originally evoked by textual stimuli (or by echoic stimuli supplied by someone reciting the list or the Veda) have come under the control of other stimuli. At least one of the latter must be present when the student or the priest begins to recite, and others are generated as the behavior proceeds. [Skinner, 1968, pp. 203-5]

A bit more recently, in *Contingencies of Reinforcement,* he stated that:

Problem solving is often said to produce knowledge. An operant formulation permits us to distinguish between some of the things to which this term has been applied.

What is knowledge, where is it, and what is it about? Michael Polanyi and P.W. Bridgman have raised these questions with respect to the apparent discrepancy between scientific facts, laws, and theories (as published, for example, in papers, texts, tables of constants, and encyclopedias) and the personal knowledge of the scientist. Objective knowledge transcends the individual; it is more stable and durable than private experience, but it lacks color and personal involvement. The presence or absence of "consciousness" can scarcely be the important difference, for scientists are as "conscious" of laws as they are of the things laws describe. Sensory contact with the external world may be the beginning of knowledge, but contact is not enough. It is not even enough for "conscious experience," since stimuli are only part of the contingencies of reinforcement under which an organism distinguishes among the aspects and properties of the environment in which it lives. Responses must be made and reinforced before anything can be seen.

The world which establishes contingencies of reinforcement of the sort studied in an operant analysis is presumably "what knowledge is about." A person comes to know that world and how to behave in it in the sense that he acquires behavior which satisfies the contingencies it maintains. Behavior which is exclusively shaped by such contingencies is perhaps the closest one can come to the "personal knowledge" of Polanyi and Bridgman. It is the directed, "purposive" behavior of the blacksmith who operates his bellows because of its effect on the fire. [Skinner, 1969. pp. 155-56]

This formulation of, and apparent solution to, the problem of knowledge cannot be known to be any more true than those that have been proposed earlier in the history of ideas. This qualification is illustrated by the persistent third question "How do we know that we know?", and it is still not clear by what means we know the means by which we know since any attempt to do so would seem to beg the question of means. Consequently, the acceptance of this proposal in place of the prior ones appears to depend on whether or not it has more utility in solving other kinds of problems than the earlier proposals, and so far it has not been given serious consideration. Perhaps now is as good a time as any to examine its implications by way of its consequences, but regardless of the outcome, the problem of knowledge will probably remain a philosophical problem of psychology.

In a rather recent appeal to psychologists for new solutions to old problems, Sigmund Koch (in Wann, ed., 1964) remarked that man is currently engaged in a sweeping redefinition of the nature of his own knowledge. This redefinition, however, has occurred primarily outside psychology among most of the other intellectual disciplines, and the methods used to accomplish it have been the traditional analytic ones. Koch's appeal apparently was for psychologists to give up the conception of knowledge they inherited from the other sciences and to formulate one more in keeping with whatever psychology has learned about the nature of knowledge. It is doubtful that the above interpretation would be endorsed by Koch since he appears to remain in the analytic traditions of the philosophy of science. Nevertheless, perhaps it is time that psychology made known what it knows about knowing, and what it knows about knowing appears to be learning.

13

The Problem of
Induction

This problem illustrates one of the fundamental limitations of science as it is currently understood. Induction, or inductive logic, provides at least some of the basis for the claim that science is empirical. However, a representative example of inductive methods, specifically induction by simple enumeration (cf. Reichenbach, 1951, p. 86), requires what might be regarded as an act of faith on the part of the scientist at the point of drawing a conclusion. In addition, there does not appear to be any way in which the methods of science can be used to eliminate that act without begging the question of induction. Hence, most if not all the empirical claims of science are based in part on faith.

Perhaps one of the earliest definitions and illustrations of induction by simple enumeration was first formulated by Aristotle (ca. 330 B.C.).

Having drawn these definitions, we must distinguish how many species there are of dialectical arguments. There is on the one hand Induction, on the other Reasoning. Now what reasoning is has been said before: induction is a passage from individuals to universals, e.g., the argument that supposing the skilled pilot is the most effective, and likewise the skilled charioteer, then in general the skilled man is the best at his particular task. Induction is the more convincing and clear: it is more readily learnt by the use of the senses, and is applicable generally to the mass of men, though Reasoning is more forcible and effective against contradictious people. [Pickard-Cambridge, 1928, p. 104]

In this formulation, the method consists of, simply, an enumeration of particular instances in which an event has occurred with, eventually, a conclusion drawn about all of them expressed in the form of a general, or universal, statement. For example, if someone finds that he suffers gastrointestinal complications on each occasion that he has eaten an unripe apple, he may eventually conclude that green apples make him sick; along with other things perhaps, he passes from particular instances to a general rule.

When he does so, however, he assumes that, were he to continue the practice, he would continue to get sick, or that the future will be like the past. That assumption is the act of faith referred to earlier and is otherwise known as the inductive leap; it is based on the assumption that nature is uniform in some, if not all, its parts, or in other words, the uniformity of nature.

This rather critical defect of induction by

enumeration was perhaps first most clearly expressed by David Hume (ca. 1740) in the abstract of his *Treatise of Human Nature*.

Here is a billiard ball lying on the table, and another ball moving toward it with rapidity. They strike; and the ball which was formerly at rest now acquires a motion. This is as perfect an instance of the relation of cause and effect as any which we know either by sensation or reflection. Let us therefore examine it. It is evident that the two balls touched one another before the motion was com-municated, and that there was no interval betwixt the shock and the motion. *Contiguity* in time and place is therefore a requisite circumstance to the operation of all causes. It is evident, likewise, that the motion which was the cause is prior to the motion which was the effect. *Priority* in time is, therefore, another requisite circumstance in every cause. But this is not all. Let us try any other balls of the same kind in a like situation, and we shall always find that the impulse of the one produces motion in the other. Here, therefore, is a *third* circumstance, viz., that of a *constant conjunction* betwixt the cause and effect. Every object like the cause produces always some object like the effect. Beyond these three circumstances of contiguity, priority, and constant conjunction I can discover nothing in this cause. The first ball is in motion, touches the second, immediately the second is in motion—and when I try the experiment with the same or like balls, in the same or like circum-stances, I find that upon the motion and touch of the one ball motion always follows in the other. In whatever shape I turn this matter, and however I examine it, I can find nothing further.

This is the case when both the cause and effect are present to the senses. Let us now see upon what our inference is founded when we conclude from the one that the other has existed or will exist. Suppose I see a ball moving in a straight line toward another—I immediately conclude that they will shock, and that the second will be in motion. This is the inference from cause to effect, and of this nature are all our reasonings in the conduct of life; on this is founded all our belief in history, and from hence is derived all philosophy excepting only geometry and arithmetic. If we can explain the inference from the shock of the two balls we shall be able to account for this operation of the mind in all instances.

Were a man such as Adam created in the full vigor of understanding, without experience, he would never be able to infer motion in the second ball from the motion and impulse of the first. It is not anything that reason sees in the cause which makes us *infer* the effect. Such an inference, were it possible, would amount to a demonstration, as being founded merely on the comparison of ideas. But no inference from cause to effect amounts to a demonstration. Of which there is this evident proof. The mind can always *conceive* any effect to follow from any cause, and indeed any event to follow upon another; whatever we *conceive* is possible, at least in a metaphysical sense; but wherever a demonstration takes place the contrary is impossible and implies a contradiction. There is no demonstration, therefore, for any conjunction of cause and effect. And this is a principle which is generally allowed by philosophers.

It would have been necessary, therefore, for Adam (if he was not inspired) to have had *experience* of the effect which followed upon the impulse of these two balls. He must have seen in several instances that when the one ball struck upon the other, the second always acquired motion. If he had seen a sufficient number of instances of this kind, whenever he saw the one ball moving toward the other, he would always conclude without hesitation that the second would acquire motion. His understanding would anticipate his sight and form a conclusion suitable to his past experience.

It follows, then, that all reasonings concerning cause and effect are founded on experience, and that all reasonings from experience are founded on the supposition that the course of nature will continue uniformly the same. We conclude that like causes, in like circumstances, will always produce like effects. It may now be worthwhile to consider what determines us to form a conclusion of such infinite consequences.

It is evident that Adam, with all his science, would never have been able to *demonstrate* that the course of nature must continue uniformly the same, and that the future must be conformable to the past. What is possible can never be demonstrated to be false; and it is possible the course of nature may change, since we can conceive such a change. Nay, I will go further and assert that he could not so much as prove by any *probable* arguments that the future must be conformable to the past. All probable arguments are built on the supposition that there is this conformity betwixt the future and the past, and therefore (he) can never prove it. This conformity is a *matter of fact*, and if it must be proved will admit of no proof but from experience. But our experience in the past can be a proof of nothing for the future but upon a supposition that there is a resemblance betwixt them. This, therefore, is a point which can admit of no proof at all, and which we take for granted without any proof. [Hume, 1955, pp. 186-89]

Stated somewhat differently, his view of induction is that it moves from particular instances to general statements about events, but when the generalization is formulated, the assumption is made that the events in question will be the same in the future as they have been in the past; that is, it is assumed that nature is uniform. However, it cannot be demonstrated that nature is uniform because a demonstrative, or deductive, argument cannot establish an inductive conclusion (or a matter of fact), and a nondemonstrative, or inductive, argument for the uniformity of nature would assume the uniformity of nature—it would beg the question. Consequently, whether or not any is required, there is no logical justification for inductive logic; it is logically invalid.

Interestingly, however, that conclusion so far has not deterred the scientist; he continues to use the methods of science and some variation on this simplest form of inductive logic to help him solve the problems with which he is confronted. As with solipsism, this state of affairs may be another instance in the history of thought in which logical analysis has led to a conclusion that was known by other means to be in error. Indeed, since logical methods have been used to explicate this conception of inductive logic, it may well be the case that a different conception, arrived at somewhat differently, may be equally instructive.

For example, there are rather striking similarities between this analysis of induction by simple enumeration and what happens during operant conditioning. If certain acts are always or only sometimes followed by certain consequences, those acts are more likely to recur in the future. Furthermore, this description seems to apply whether or not the organism that performs them enumerates particular instances of what he has done and then draws a general conclusion about them as required by a logical analysis of his performance. It may be that a logical reconstruction of behavior is, as the history of both philosophy and psychology amply suggests, totally at variance with how organisms, in fact, behave, especially with regard to how they draw conclusions (if they do).

Aside from Aristotle and Hume, others have exhibited an interest in this problem. For example, Francis Bacon (ca. 1620) was highly critical of induction by simple enumeration as it was known in his time and proposed an alternative to it.

In forming axioms, we must invent a different form of induction from that hitherto in use; not only for the proof and discovery of principles (as they are called), but also of minor, intermediate, and, in short, every kind of axioms. The induction which proceeds by simple enumeration is puerile, leads to uncertain conclusions, and is exposed to danger from one contradictory instance, deciding generally from too small a number of facts, and those only the most obvious. But a really useful induction for the discovery and demonstration of the arts and sciences, should separate nature by proper rejections and exclusions, and then conclude for the affirmative, after collecting a sufficient number of negatives. Now this has not been done, nor even attempted, except perhaps by Plato, who certainly uses this form of induction in some measure, to sift definitions and ideas. But much of what has never yet entered the thoughts of man must necessarily be employed, in order to exhibit a good and legitimate mode of induction or demonstration, so as even to render it essential for us to bestow more pains upon it than have hitherto been bestowed on syllogisms. The assistance of induction is to serve us not only in the discovery of axioms, but also in defining our notions. Much indeed is to be hoped from such an induction as has been described. [Bacon, 1900, p. 353]

The alternative method of positive and negative instances proposed by Bacon was not remarkably different from induction by simple enumeration and, as is well known, was offered as a means of avoiding errors of thought that he referred to as idols of the tribe, den, market, and theater.

Similarly, John Stuart Mill (ca. 1843) was cognizant of the problem and proposed his own alternatives to the method of induction by simple enumeration.

The induction of the ancients has been well described by Bacon, under the name of "Inductio per enumerationem simplicem, ubi non reperitur

instantia contradictoria." It consists in ascribing
the character of general truths to all propositions
which are true in every instance that we happen to
know of. This is the kind of induction which is
natural to the mind when unaccustomed to scientific methods. The tendency, which some call an
instinct, and which others account for by association, to infer the future from the past, the unknown
from the known, is simply a habit of expecting that
what has been found true once or several times,
and never yet found false, will be found true again.
Whether the instances are few or many, conclusive
or inconclusive, does not much affect the matter:
these are considerations which occur only on
reflection; the unprompted tendency of the mind
is to generalise its experience, provided this points
all in one direction; provided no other experience
of a conflicting character comes unsought. The
notion of seeking it, of experimenting for it, of
interrogating nature (to use Bacon's expression) is
of much later growth. The observation of nature
by uncultivated intellects is purely passive: they
accept the facts which present themselves,
without taking the trouble of searching for more: it
is a superior mind only which asks itself what facts
are needed to enable it to come to a safe
conclusion, and then looks out for these.

But though we have always a propensity to
generalize from unvarying experience, we are not
always warranted in doing so. Before we can be at
liberty to conclude that something is universally
true because we have never known an instance to
the contrary, we must have reason to believe that if
there were in nature any instances to the contrary,

we should have known of them. This assurance, in the great majority of cases, we cannot have, or can have only in a very moderate degree. The possibility of having it is the foundation on which we shall see hereafter that induction by simple enumeration may in some remarkable cases amount practically to proof. No such assurance, however, can be had on any of the ordinary subjects of scientific inquiry. Popular notions are usually founded on induction by simple enumeration; in science it carries us but a little way. We are forced to begin with it; we must often rely on it provisionally, in the absence of means of more searching investigation. But, for the accurate study of nature, we require a surer and a more potent instrument. [Mill, 1936, p. 204]

The "surer and more potent instrument[s]" that he proposed were the methods of agreement, difference, residues, concomitant variations, and a combination of the first two.

Other more recent authors have not left the problem unattended. For example, Katz (1962) pointed out not only that the problem is still a viable one for many philosophers but also that the justification of induction cannot be separated from the problem of induction.

Hume argued that conclusions arrived at by induction cannot be justified by any of the methods of justification common in the mathematical sciences, since inductive conclusions are, unlike those drawn from mathematical arguments, at best highly probable, never certain. He argued further that such conclusions cannot be justified by appealing to what we have found in past experience, since any appeal to experience would involve an inference from the past to the future and would *ipso facto* beg the very question at issue. Hume sought some other way to justify induction but could find none. Consequently, he left the problem in this form. Since Hume's work, many philosophers tried without success to discover a justification of induction which would escape Hume's skeptical arguments, and others attempted with equal lack of success to prove that the task of justifying induction is, as Hume strongly suspected, an impossible one. Numerous arguments were offered on each side of the issue, but pitifully few turned out to be substantive, and none proved conclusive. From Kant, who was the first philosopher to consider the problem seriously, to Reichenbach, who with the possible exception of Peirce, was the first to make a substantive contribution to it, many of the most influential philosophers in modern philosophy— Russell, Wittgenstein, Keynes, Ramsey—have grappled with the problem. But the problem has remained as much a riddle as Hume left it. [Katz, 1962, pp. ix-x]

At a later point in his discussion, Katz claimed to solve the problem of justification negatively. That is, he concluded that there is no way in which induction can be either validated or even vindicated on the pragmatic basis that it works; for him, there was not even a prospect for the justification of induction.

The matter of justification appears to be related to traditional rationalism, which was discussed earlier in relation to the various kinds of explanation in psychology. According to traditional rationalism, to explain an action or a practice is to give the reasons for it, and, apparently, to justify it is to do likewise. Consequently, to justify induction seems to require that the reasons for it be stated, which means that it be made consistent with some set of logical, or rational, premises. However, such an effort is necessary only if it is granted that induction requires justification; traditional rationalism may do so, but some other mode of explanation may not. Thus far, induction has not been justified on a rational basis, which suggests that perhaps it cannot be. Nevertheless, the uniformity of nature assumption may require some refinement, as illustrated in the following remark by Bertrand Russell (1912, pp. 97-98).

> A horse which has been often driven along a certain road resists the attempt to drive him in a different direction. Domestic animals expect food when they see the person who usually feeds them. We know that all these rather crude expectations of uniformity are liable to be misleading. The man who has fed the chicken every day throughout its life at last wrings its neck instead, showing that more refined views as to the uniformity of nature would have been useful to the chicken.

14

The Fact-Value Problem

This problem is perhaps the most intricate of those that have been examined so far. The most frequent formulation of it has to do with the difference between statements of fact and statements of value. For philosophers, the problem is how statements of fact can lead to statements of value..But, for psychologists, the issue may be whether, in fact, statements of fact differ from statements of value; that is, whether it has ever been shown with the methods of science that these two kinds of statements are, in fact, different.

Many authors have had occasion to write on this problem, only a few of whom will be mentioned in a brief review of its history in philosophy and psychology. As with so many of the other philosophical problems of psychology, this one may be traced back to Socrates and the beginnings of ethical philosophy in the fifth century B.C. However, it was apparently the Sophists who "stressed the difference between subjective values and objective facts, arguing that good and evil are matters of personal decision or social agreement *(nomos)* rather than facts of nature *(phusis)*" (Abelson and Neilsen, 1967, p. 82). Socrates apparently did not distinguish between judgments of value and judgments of fact; that distinction was perhaps first made explicit in more recent times by David Hume and stressed by G.E. Moore. However, it may have been Socrates who first suggested the dichotomy, rather inadvertently, when he made reference to two logically separated realms of statements eventually developed by Plato into a realm of substance and a realm of ideas or forms (Abelson and Nielsen, 1967, pp. 82-83).

David Hume (ca. 1737), to whom both philosophy and pyschology owe so much for clarifying many of their respective and mutual philosophical problems, concluded that it was not possible to deduce an *ought*, or matter of value, from an *is* or matter of fact. For example, in the closing paragraph to the third book, the first part, and the first section of his *Treatise of Human Nature*, Hume (1888, pp. 469-70) stated that he could not

> forbear adding to these reasonings an observation, which may, perhaps, be found of some importance. In every system of morality, which I have hitherto met with, I have always remark'd, that the author proceeds for some time in the ordinary way of reasoning, and establishes the being of a God, or makes observations concerning human affairs; when of a sudden I am surpriz'd to find, that instead of the usual copulations of propositions, *is*,

and *is not,* I meet with no proposition that is not connected with an *ought,* or an *ought not.* This change is imperceptible; but is, however, of the last consequence. For as this *ought,* or *ought not,* expresses some new relation or affirmation, 'tis necessary that it shou'd be observ'd and explain'd; and at the same time that a reason should be given, for what seems altogether inconceivable, how this new relation can be a deduction from others, which are entirely different from it. But as authors do not commonly use this precaution, I shall presume to recommend it to the readers; and am persuaded, that this small attention wou'd subvert all the vulgar systems of morality, and let us see, that the distinction of vice and virtue is not founded merely on the relation of objects, nor is perceiv'd by reason.

Interestingly, this conclusion was arrived at primarily by way of a rational, rather than an empirical, analysis of the problem even though Hume was known as a British empiricist.

Some time later, G.E. Moore (ca. 1903) argued that values were not natural properties of things or events and that any attempt to define them as natural properties was a mistake, which he referred to as "the naturalistic fallacy." For example, in his *Principia Ethica,* Moore (1959, p. 10) asked his reader to

Consider yellow, for example. We may try to define it, by describing its physical equivalent; we may state what kind of light-vibrations must stimulate the normal eye, in order that we may perceive it. But a moment's reflection is sufficient to show that those light-vibrations are not themselves what we mean by yellow. *They* are not what we perceive. Indeed we should never have been able to discover their existence, unless we had first been struck by the patent difference of quality between the different colours. The most we can be entitled to say of those vibrations is that they are what corresponds in space to the yellow which we actually perceive.

Yet a mistake of this simple kind has commonly been made about 'good.' It may be true that all things which are good are *also* something else, just as it is true that all things which are yellow produce a certain kind of vibration in the light. And it is a fact, that Ethics aims at discovering what are those other properties belonging to all things which are good. But far too many philosophers have thought that when they named those other properties they were actually defining good; that these properties, in fact, were simply not 'other,' but absolutely and entirely the same with goodness. This view I propose to call the 'naturalistic fallacy' . . . .

His subsequent discussion argued that good was indefinable, but at least one thing that it was not was a natural property of objects or events, although it might, nevertheless, be a property of objects or events.

Perhaps enough instances have been cited from the history of the fact-value problem in philosophy to suggest that at least some philosophers of the first rank accepted the disjunction between facts and values without much question. However, their basis for doing so was largely analytic, or rational, rather than empirical. Those few psychologists who have concerned themselves with the problem seem to have adopted somewhat different views.

For example, Edward L. Thorndike (1936, p. 2) stated that

> judgments of value are simply one sort of judgments of fact, distinguished from the rest by two characteristics; they concern consequences. These are consequences to the wants of sentient beings. Values, positive and negative, reside in the satisfaction or annoyance felt by animals, persons or deities. If the occurrence of X can have no influence on the satisfaction or discomfort of anyone present or future, X has no value, is neither good nor bad, desirable nor undesirable. Values are functions of preferences. Judgments about values—statements that A is good, B is bad, C is right, D is useful—refer ultimately to satisfactions or annoyances in sentient creatures and depend upon their preferences. Competent students judge the existence of things by observations of them; they judge the values of things by observations of their consequences.

Thus, for Thorndike, value judgments were simply another kind of factual judgment that was based on the consequences of things or events for creatures capable of sensation. Nonetheless, a distinction could be made between them and other kinds of factual judgments.

Similarly, Wolfgang Kohler (1938, pp. 102-3) reasoned that:

> To find the place of values in a world of facts is a

task which has two different sides. First, there is
the problem of principle: If experience gives us
facts, how, in the same experience, can we find a
place for requiredness? Like all questions of fundamental principle this problem can only be
solved on phenomenological grounds. In a
preliminary way it seems to be solved by the observation that "fact" is an ambiguous term, that not
all facts are "indifferent facts," and that within
certain factual contexts the requiredness or
wrongness of some facts is no less real than is the
existence of these facts. We have thus given to
values a logical place among the facts. The second
side of our task refers to a question of distribution.
Experience in general has many domains. Where
among these do we find requiredness as a
characteristic of definite contexts? Until now our
approach had to be phenomenological, so that the
term "requiredness" could be given a definite
meaning. Such a restriction is no longer necessary.
Phenomenology is the field in which all concepts
find their final justification. To what fields such
concepts may be applied, once their meaning has
been elucidated, is another question. And it is the
aim of the next chapters to decide whether
requiredness as we have now defined it has any
place outside the phenomenal realm.

In those chapters, it was decided that there was a
correspondence, more accurately an isomorphism,
between phenomenal requiredness and the neural
events produced by their counterparts in nature. However, toward the close of his essay, he concluded that
not much had been accomplished by it except perhaps

that it had shown how science might deal with questions of value if only in an illustrative way and that it had helped to overcome difficulties of principle that might facilitate further advance. Nevertheless, values were given "a logical place among the facts."

More recently, in a chapter of *Beyond Freedom and Dignity* entitled simply "Values," B.F. Skinner (1971, pp. 104-26) argued that

> When we say that a value judgment is a matter not of fact but of how someone feels about a fact, we are simply distinguishing between a thing and its reinforcing effect. Things themselves are studied by physics and biology, usually without reference to their value, but the reinforcing effects of things are the province of behavioral science, which, to the extent that it is concerned with operant reinforcement, is a science of values. [p. 104]

> Once we have identified the contingencies that control the behavior called good or bad and right or wrong, the distinction between facts and how people feel about facts is clear. How people feel about facts is a by-product. The important thing is what they do about them, and what they do is a fact that is to be understood by examining relevant contingencies. . . . [p. 113]

Thus, for Skinner, as for Thorndike, values are matters of fact for a science of behavior that are related to the consequences of behavior; they are, therefore, explained by those consequences. Values are facts of behavior to be explained by a science of behavior.

This very brief review of the fact-value problem in the history of both philosophy and psychology suggests that even if it were a matter of fact that statements of fact differed from statements of value, it probably could not be known that they were, in any definitive way, with the methods of science; those methods do not provide definitive answers. If they did, the problem of metaphysics, for example, probably would have been resolved by this time, but since it has not, the fact-value problem may suffer a similar fate.

This situation may help to explain how it happens that statements of fact have been considered different from statements of value by philosophers such as the Sophists, Hume, and Moore. It may also help to explain how statements of value have been equated with statements of fact by psychologists such as Thorndike, Kohler, and Skinner.

There are at least two more ways in which those statements might be treated. The first is that statements of fact might be equated with statements of value, and the second is that all statements formerly viewed either as fact or as value might be considered to have both a factual and an evaluative component. There are, thus, at least four possible ways to treat this problem: fact and value statements may be different; they both may be facts; they both may be values; or they both may contain factual and evaluative components. However, what they are really, or in some absolute sense, probably cannot be known with the methods of science, since the products of those methods are always, so far as can be known, probable.

Another factor that may prevent a resolution of the fact-value problem with the methods of science is that, no matter how the problem is formulated, it may beg the question in favor of one or the other side of the issue. In other words, the way in which the problem is formulated may presuppose a certain basis on which it is to be resolved, which may predispose the inquiry toward one kind of solution rather than another as seems to have been the case with the philosophers and psychologists referred to above. Such considerations are no more true of this kind of inquiry than of any other, but they may be especially cogent with respect to this philosophical problem of psychology.

If facts and values were treated as equivalent, it might happen that discussions could no longer be terminated with the utterance, so frequently encountered when policy decisions are being made, "But, that is a matter of value!" Such an utterance usually terminates the discussion because "everyone knows" that there is no way of resolving differences about matters of value. However, if values are simply a function of the consequences of behavior as suggested by a science of values, then to resolve matters of value requires simply some reference to the consequences of particular behaviors as well as the effects they have on subsequent behaviors, that is, some reference to the laws of behavior. But, since that conclusion undoubtedly may require some time before it becomes more generally accepted, this analysis of the fact-value problem seems to show rather clearly that, for now, the distinction between facts and values may not be a matter of fact so much as it is a matter of convention.

15

Conclusion

Scholarship on the philosophical problems of psychology continues, and, consequently, it cannot be supposed that they finally have been dispensed with in this rather brief review. Aside from stating what they are and how they have been treated in the past for a general audience composed of psychologists and other students of psychology, perhaps all that has been accomplished is simply that some of the more salient of them have been presented and discussed as philosophical problems of psychology; however, many of them are no more problems for psychology than they are for any of the other sciences. The future may show that the effort expended to resolve them now and in the past has been wasted, but it may also reveal that such effort is, or was, propaedeutic to the evolution of a science of behavior.

Conclusion

Nevertheless, many of them will probably continue to flourish for some time as significant problems for psychology in the common sense approach to the understanding of human and animal behavior; it need hardly be said that common sense solutions have a rather broad basis of support, in the form of positive reinforcement, among those only casually acquainted with problems of this sort. Common sense has its defenders, and there is probably nothing basically wrong with it; it may well be one of those behaviors that have led to the survival of the species. However, it does not just occur; it is shaped by the past. For example, Descartes and the scholastic philosophers before him came to give man a mind and body several hundred years ago, and today "everyone knows" that bodily actions are explained by the mental events that sometimes, but not always, precede them, although the mental events tend to remain unexplained. Similarly, "everyone knows" there is a real world that is discovered by science, although that world is known only by means of sense experience, and, hence, that it is sense experience and not necessarily a real world that is known by science. Common sense solutions may have helped, but they can also hinder, the development of a science, especially one that originated in, and eventually will have to explain if it cannot now do so, common sense behavior itself.

The discussion of these problems simply could terminate at this point with what has been presented and with no claim that they finally have been resolved; they persist and probably will continue to do so for as long as there are those who raise questions about the philosophical aspects of psychology. There may be some who are tempted to conclude that these problems have been examined much in the fashion of the philosopher who first stirred up the dust and then complained that he could not see; perhaps that is as much as can be done with them at the present time. However, what has been presented suggests that these problems continue to be of relevance to contemporary psychology.

For example, the mind-body problem is relevant to contemporary psychology to the extent that the dualistic nature of man remains unchallenged. However, when it is no longer granted that he is composed of two unlike substances that govern or regulate one another, or that the inner man is different from the outer one, or that what goes on inside man is more important in explaining his behavior than what goes on outside him, the problem vanishes. What remains is the somewhat more parsimonious proposition that there are some things men do that can be observed directly and others that cannot. Nevertheless, the observed and unobserved are basically the same kind of event, namely, behavior; some are overt and some are covert. Neither is more important than the other in explaining behavior since they are both behavior to be explained by the variables related to them.

This treatment of mind neither affirms nor denies its existence. As with any other concept developed by man, there does not appear to be any empirical test that, if performed, would either confirm or not confirm the existence of whatever it is that the concept is supposed to denote. There is no more empirical evidence against mind than there is for it. While no one has ever seen, heard, felt, tasted, or smelled mind, neither has it been demonstrated that one could not. Consequently, the early somewhat radical behaviorists were in no better position to affirm mind than they were to deny it. The evolution of behavioral science might have proceeded more smoothly if J.B. Watson, for example, had been interpreted as mute on the question of the existence of mind, but, rather, had evaluated it on the basis of its utility. The judgment of contemporary psychology seems to be that mind is not a particularly useful concept for an empirical explanation of behavior, although it will probably continue to be found useful for a common sense one.

The problem of metaphysics, or ontology, is relevant to contemporary psychology because, although the question of what there is may not be answered explicitly by the psychologist, it may be answered implicitly by the way in which he phrases statements about his observations. The textbook language of psychology today is based largely on a realistic ontology, and many psychologists, as well as students of psychology, would probably agree that psychologists as scientists discover the phenomena and laws of the universe in the behavioral laboratory. It may well be the case that they do, but they cannot know that they do since what is known by means of all present empirical procedures is sense experience and not necessarily a real world that exists independently of it. The phenomena and laws of behavior could just as well be developed or constructed, as discovered, in the experimental laboratory.

It is of some interest that the discussion on metaphysics is so short. That circumstance may be explained by the fact that nearly all of the problems examined are, perhaps, simply different aspects of that one problem or else originate from it. For example, the mind-body problem arises only if it is granted that man is composed of more than one substance; that assumption is often classified as metaphysical. Similarly, the problem of theory arises when it is assumed that a theory is a true representation of a real state of affairs rather than a logical construction of sense experience. Once again, such an assumption may be called metaphysical, and different assumptions of this kind may be said to occur with other problems such as reification, causality, and purpose, to name only a few of the most obvious. Consequently, and with some justification, it might be concluded that the entire discussion of all of these problems is metaphysics and, hence, that what appears to be the shortest analysis is in fact the longest since it is related in some way to nearly every problem that has been examined.

Reification is relevant to contemporary psychology so long as it continues to be based on a realistic ontology; the problem arises when words are used to denote things rather than, or in addition to, sense experience. When words are used in at least these two ways, it frequently is difficult to determine which one of them is intended. For example, the word *mind* could be used to denote some rather contradictory "unextended but thinking substance" or it could be used to denote simply the observed functions of the brain. How it is interpreted, or is to be interpreted, depends in part upon the ontological position of the user as well as that of his audience.

The ontology of phenomenalism is not without its own special problems. One of them, and perhaps the most important, is solipsism, or the egocentric predicament, as it has also been called. A somewhat modernized version of it is as follows: If all that is or can be known is sense experience, and if all that anyone can know is his own sense experience, then scientific knowledge is not possible since it is based on the sense experience of observers and not just one of them. However, scientific knowledge, or at least what we call it, is possible, and consequently there is something wrong with phenomenalism, the logic, our conception of knowledge, or all three.

There have been many occasions in the history of ideas when logic has led to a conclusion that was known by other means to be in error. Perhaps the most famous, aside from the antinomies of Kant, is the paradox of Zeno. He was faced with the dilemma of hitting a target with an arrow when between the target and the arrow, or for that matter between the arrow and the bowstring, there was an infinite series of points. Since an infinite series of points has neither a beginning nor an end, it logically was not possible for Zeno even to begin to shoot the arrow let alone hit the target. The arrow quivering at its destination suggests once more that there is something wrong with the premises, the logic, or what we claim to know about an observed state of affairs; the discussion of how the problem of knowledge is relevant to contemporary psychology, which appears later, may help to place this special philosophical problem of psychology into a somewhat different perspective.

The problems of explanation and causality are relevant to contemporary psychology to the extent that psychologists and students of psychology continue to require and are provided with causal explanations in some form other than functional relationships. It is initially rather difficult to accept the statement that behavioral events are explained by the variables of which they are a function because such explanations do not appear to answer the question "Why?" However, closer examination of that question, at least when it is asked of a science, reveals that functional relationships do answer it, probably, since absolute truth does not emerge from applications of the methodology of science.

The problems of theory, laws, and principles, as well as knowledge, are relevant to contemporary psychology because, without some formal examination of them such as has occurred here, there may be no occasion for those who are only casually interested in psychology to consider the possibility that psychological theories, laws, or principles, and human knowledge in general, are neither true nor false. An exception may appear to be those statements regarded as theories, or knowledge, that are true on a logical, or analytic, basis. However, as the history of rationalism rather copiously suggests, it is not always possible to confirm on an empirical basis what may be true on a logical one.

The methods of science as they are currently understood, and that understanding is by no means complete, provide theories or knowledge that simply is probable and not necessarily true in some absolute sense; even if they were true in that sense, it apparently cannot be known that they are. Consequently, it seems that their acceptance as matters of fact depends not only on whatever probabilities can be attached to them but also on how useful, or heuristic, they are in the integration of what has already been learned as well as in the prediction of outcomes to be put to empirical test. On the other hand, the examination of that problem indicates that perhaps a new conception of knowledge is emerging that is quite different from the conception of knowledge that psychology inherited from the other sciences and the philosophy of science. Nevertheless, that conception is consistent with the view of psychology as the science of behavior.

The problem of laws and principles is relevant to contemporary psychology not only because it is so closely related to the problem of theory but also because there are those who still regard the laws and principles of a science as fixed and immutable characteristics of nature obeyed by things and events in it. Indeed, there are many who would argue that probable laws and principles cannot be scientific laws and principles at all because they may have to be modified as more evidence emerges from empirical investigations. However, the view of laws and principles as representing fixed and immutable factors obeyed by things and events in nature appears to be based on a realistic ontology that may have to be given up as more is learned about science and what it is able to do.

The problem of anthropomorphism is of relevance to contemporary psychology because it still may occur even among those who recognize it as a problem. Its occurrence, however, may not be an error or a fallacy so much as it represents a lack of parsimony in explanations of behavior; it may unnecessarily overcomplicate them. In addition, anthropomorphic explanations appear to be untestable. It apparently cannot be known whether animals have human characteristics or whether humans have animal characteristics since, in either case, they are probably human constructions. In that respect, it may be as parsimonious to treat both animals and humans as having human characteristics as to treat them both as having animal characteristics. For now, however, the admonition to eschew anthropomorphism may have to suffice since there apparently are few psychologists who would entertain that possibility. Nevertheless, it could happen that, at some future time, anthropomorphism will once again become fashionable because, while there is apparently no valid reason to suppose that animals have human characteristics, there is likewise none to suppose they do not; the question of the characteristics to be found in either is still an open one. Hence, the kind of anthropomorphism practiced in the future, if there ever is one, may be quite different from that against which Lloyd Morgan aimed his canon.

Contemporary psychology seems to be moving away from anthropomorphic explanations of behavior. However, that movement may be in the direction of mechanomorphism and a second form of what was referred to earlier as zoomorphism; the first form is the assignment, by animals, of animal characteristics to humans, and the second form is the assignment, by humans, of animal characteristics to other humans. Apparently, it has not yet been generally accepted that human behavior is not explained by reference to either animal, or human, or mechanical characteristics but by reference to its laws. And, until that acceptance occurs, psychologists and students of psychology may have to be admonished to eschew not only anthropomorphism and mechanomorphism but zoomorphism as well.

The problem of purpose is relevant to contemporary psychology because the concept does not seem to have been critically evaluated by a sufficient number of psychologists. Many appear simply to have accepted purpose, and goal direction, as basic facts of behavior when it may not have been necessary to do so. Purpose and goal direction may be no more facts of behavior than they are simply features of our traditional ways of attempting to conceptualize behavior; they may be dictated less by what is observed than by our unexamined "theories of ourselves" (cf. Koch, 1956, pp. 60-61).

Common sense may require that behavior be purposive when a host of other concepts may be more fruitful in explaining it. One of them is reinforcement (cf. Skinner, 1969, p. 125), but it needs to be recognized that the language of reinforcement itself eventually may prove to be as limited as that of purpose. It does not now seem likely that any science, behavioral or otherwise, will ever reach that point at which further modification of its concepts will no longer occur. The conceptual schemes peculiar to a science probably will always undergo revision as more is learned by those who practice the science.

The problem of freedom is relevant to contemporary psychology because apparently it continues to challenge every generation of psychologists. However, it may be more relevant on a political basis than a scientific one. In a society such as that in which American psychology has evolved, the political problem of freedom appears to be whether, in principle, men are free to act, and within certain legal limits specified by the Constitution and the courts, they are. On the other hand, for a science of behavior the problem of freedom is whether, in fact, men are free to act, and so far no instances have been found in which they are. However, the failure to find such instances does not mean there are none. It may mean either that no one has searched for them or that the methods of science can be used to determine only that men are not free rather than that they are.

The problem of knowledge is also relevant to contemporary psychology in a somewhat different way than that discussed in connection with the problem of theory. The problem has been a persistent one in the history of ideas, and it undoubtedly will continue to be one for some time to come. However, psychology may have more to say about knowledge than what it has said and what has been said by philosophers of science. For many philosophers of science and a great number of psychologists, we know by means of the methodology of science as it has been explicated by philosophers of science. For many other psychologists, however, the problem of knowledge may be not "By what means do we know?" but, rather, "How does it comes about that we know?" and the answer to that question appears to be "What has been learned about learning."

This treatment of knowledge may help to place some related philosophical problems of psychology into a somewhat different perspective; they are the problem of objectivity and the problem of solipsism. At an early period in the history of science, the problem of objectivity was how man could know nature uncontaminated with his presuppositions about nature, as though nature was there simply waiting to be known. In addition, it was felt that the methods of science allowed men to know nature in that unbiased way. With the advent of logical positivism and philosophy of science, objectivity in science became intersubjective testability, which meant that the results of an experiment, for example, were objective if they could be replicated by competent observers. However, when knowledge is treated as learning rather than as something that is acquired by the methods of science, the problem of objectivity is no longer a significant one, since what men learn is not knowledge but what is shaped into their behavior by those contingencies of reinforcement that affect that behavior; men do not acquire something called knowledge but, rather, different behaviors.

The related problem of solipsism is also no longer a significant one with this treatment of knowledge. As noted earlier, a somewhat modernized version of this problem is that, if all that can be known is sense experience, and if all that anyone can know is his own sense experience, then scientific knowledge is not possible since it is based on the sense experience of observers and not just one of them. Apparently, this problem arises from a logical, or rational, analysis of what must be the case if the metaphysical or ontological position of phenomenalism is true. However, neither phenomenalism nor realism can be known to be true with the empirical methods of science as they are currently understood, and so solipsism ceases to be a significant problem on that basis alone. Aside from that, it is entirely possible for phenomenalism to be empirically true but the logical implications from it to be false. Indeed, both phenomenalism and solipsism could be true, both could be false, or one could be false and the other true on either an empirical or a rational basis. But, regardless of these considerations, men know, and what they know, as well as how they know it, is explained not by logic but by the laws and principles of learning when knowledge is treated as learning.

The problem of induction is of continued relevance to contemporary psychology because inductive logic appears to be of central importance to the methodology of science, and since psychology has adopted that methodology, any problem with induction is a problem for psychology. However, induction apparently can be neither validated nor even vindicated on either a logical or a pragmatic basis, which means that the behavioral scientist is using methods that are not philosophically justifiable but that he, the scientist, cannot do without. Under such circumstances, he might be tempted to conclude "so much the worse for philosophy"; an alternative is to question whether justification is required.

Finally, the fact-value problem is relevant to contemporary psychology because behavioral science is so closely related to what men do as well as to what they ought to do. In the past, the former has been treated as a matter of fact and left to science, whereas the latter has been treated as a matter of value and left to ethics. However, the difference itself may not be a matter of fact so much as it is a matter of convention, which implies that other conventions with respect to the problem might be adopted. The one suggested by a science of behavior, or a science of values, is to treat them both as matters of fact. To do so might, in turn, contribute to the solution of problems, in addition to those examined here, that traditionally have been considered philosophical and, hence, unresolvable.

It is perhaps of some importance to note that there may be an element of convention in nearly every statement that men make, if only the conventions of the language in which such statements are expressed. However, it may be of greater importance that many of the philosophical problems of a science appear to be resolved, or perhaps dispensed with, by way of conventions arrived at by those who practice the science. If so, the solutions to the philosophical problems of a science may change as the conventions of its scientists change. One implication of that possibility is that individual scientists may actively engage in changing the conventions of their science; what has been presented here may be a step in that direction. The effect might be to hasten the evolution of a science of behavior with a conception of science appropriate to its subject matter rather than one patterned after a view of science explicated by the philosophers of science.

This discussion of some thirteen philosophical problems of psychology does not necessarily exhaust the supply, although the ones that remain may not be as salient as those examined at this time. For many psychologists, these problems all may be "relics of a bygone age." However, each new generation of college students and those who develop only a casual interest in psychology seem to require that they be examined and resolved anew; perhaps this discussion will help to facilitate that process.

Glossary

The words included here are defined according to how they are used in the text. The definitions express the common usage of the words in both philosophy and psychology. However, the reader is cautioned that such definitions do not include all of the possible nuances of meaning that may be found for these words in both areas of inquiry.

Animisn. The belief that all things are animated or possess a spirit.

Anthropomorphism. The assignment of human characteristics to animals.

Antinomy. A logical paradox such as the statement that all statements are wrong.

Axiom. A self-evident proposition.

Behaviorism. The view that the subject matter of

psychology is the behavior of organisms and is to be studied with observational methods.

Common sense solutions. What "everyone knows."

Construct. A word used to represent a number of observations.

Constructive explanation. An interpretation of events by means of constructs.

Contiguity. The space or time proximity of events; for example, thunder is contiguous with lightning.

Correlation. The relation between two dependent variables; R-R law; as one varies the other varies, affording prediction but not control.

Cosmogony. A pictoral view of how the world or universe originated.

Cosmology. The study of the origin and structure of the universe.

Cybernetics. The study of messages and feedback, or control, systems.

Deductive logic. The logical method that proceeds from general to particular statements according to certain rules of logic.

Dependent variable. Some measure of behavior such as frequency or rate of response.

Determinism. The view that all events are determined, or made to occur, by prior events.

Dialectical argument. A form of argumentation that involves a thesis, antithesis, and synthesis.

Double-aspect hypothesis. The view that mind and body are simply two aspects of the same "stuff," thing, or underlying reality.

Dualism. Any view that presupposes two basic elements whatever they might be.

Dualistic materialism. Any view that presupposes two basic substances.

Ego-centric predicament. The situation that is said to occur if all that can be known is one's own sense experience. Events that are not experienced cannot be known; the experience of others does not count.

Emergentism. The view that objects or events have emergent properties in combination, which cannot be predicted from their separate properties.

Empirical. Observational; of the senses.

Epiphenomenalism. The solution to the mind-body problem that treats mind as an epiphenomenon or an event that is an effect but has no effects.

Epistemology. Theory of knowledge; the study of the origin, nature, and limitations of knowledge.

Ethics. The study of correct, or right, conduct.

Ethologist. One who studies animal behavior with naturalistic methods.

Experimental analysis of behavior. Another name for operant conditioning.

Explanation. Interpretation; a statement in which the event to be explained is related to other similar events described by a law.

Functional relation. So-called causal relation between independent and dependent variables; S-R law. As one is varied, the other varies, affording prediction and control.

Gestalt psychology. The view of psychology in which the "form quality" of perceptual events is of major importance.

179

Heuristic. Useful in stimulating research.

Homunculus. Little man within something, usually another man.

Hylozoism. The view that matter is alive.

Hypostatize. To reify; to treat as things, things that are not things.

Hypothesis. An untested statement about how something works or happens.

Hypothetical construct. A theoretical device used to represent the empirical relationship between measured variables and the mechanism that might account for it; an intervening variable with "surplus meaning."

Idealism. The position that stresses ideas, ideals, mind, or spirit.

Identity hypothesis. A solution to the mind-body problem that identifies mind with body or body with mind.

Independent variable. Something to which behavior may be related, such as food or water deprivation.

Inductive logic. The logical method that moves from particular to general statements according to certain rules of logic.

Instantiation. A type of explanation in which the event explained is said to be an instance of others described by a law.

Interactionism. A solution to the mind-body problem in which it is asserted that mind and body interact even though they are different substances.

Intervening variable. A theoretical device used to represent the empirical relationship between measured variables.

Introspectionism. A tradition in psychology that emphasizes introspection, or a looking within at subjective experience, as an observational method.

Isomorphism. The Gestalt doctrine of a one-to-one correspondence between a stimulus and the areas of the cerebral cortex excited by it.

Law. A statement of a relationship between variables, such as frequency of reinforcement and rate of responding.

Libido. Freudian conception for what energizes the personality; sexuality.

Logical analyst. A philosopher or philosopher of science concerned with the logical analysis of language.

Logical positivism. The philosophical position that stresses the logical analysis of, and positive evidence for, scientific knowledge.

Materialism. Any position that places major importance on matter, substance, or body.

Mechanomorphism. The assignment of mechanical characteristics to humans.

Mentalism. The position that humans have mental characteristics.

Metaphysics. That branch of philosophy that studies the nature of knowledge, or epistemology, and the nature of being, or ontology.

Meta-theory. A theory of theory.

Molar-molecular. Distinction between macro- and micro-elements, especially of behavior; walking is molar relative to the knee reflex, which is molecular.

Monadology. The view of the German philosopher Liebniz that the monad is the elementary unit of the universe.

Monism. Any doctrine that emphasizes one "stuff," whether mind, or body, or something else.

Narcissism. Self-love.

Nativism-empiricism. Distinction between inborn and acquired characteristics of perceptual experience.

Naturalistic fallacy. The mistaken notion that values are natural properties of objects or events.

Nature-nurture. Distinction between inborn and acquired behavior of organisms.

Nominal fallacy. The mistaken notion that to name something is to explain it.

Occasionalism. A solution to the mind-body problem which assumes that a deity intervenes on those occasions when mind influences body or body influences mind.

Ontology. The study of the nature of being or reality.

Operant. An emitted behavior.

Operant conditioning. A technique for modifying emitted behavior.

Operational definition. A definition in which a term is defined by what a scientist does when he uses it.

Parallelism. The position that events in one realm parallel those in another, but there is no interaction between them.

Parsimony. The conception, sometimes referred to as a law or principle, that the simplest explanation is the preferred one.

Phenomenalism. The metaphysical, or ontological, position that the basic given in the universe is sense experience.

Phenomenology. The study of phenomena as they are confronted in naive experience rather than through trained introspection.

Philosophical problem. A problem that cannot be solved with the methods of science.

Philosophy of science. A statement of what it is that science is about or what science does.

Physicalism. The view that all scientific knowledge can be expressed in the language of physical science.

Positivism. The position that requires positive evidence for scientific knowledge.

Pragmatist. One who stresses the practicality or utility of knowledge.

Principle. A general statement based on laws.

Propaedeutic. Preliminary; introductory.

Psychophysical dualism. A position that asserts two of whatever is asserted, specifically a psychical and a physical.

Psychophysical parallelism. A solution to the mind-body problem in which it is said that mind parallels body, but they do not interact.

Psychophysics. The study of the relations between the psychical and the physical, or mind and body, or sensation and stimulus, or response and stimulus.

Rationalism. The view that all knowledge is obtained by reason or rationality.

Realism. The metaphysical, or ontological, position that a real world exists independently of any observer.

Reductionism. The belief that all of the sciences can be reduced to one, namely, physics.

Reductive explanation. A type of explanation in which events at one level are interpreted as events at another, such as learning and synaptic changes.

Reification. The treatment of words as though they referred to things; behavior has been reified if it is assumed that the word refers to some thing.

Reinforcement. What happens when a stimulus condition produced by a response increases its frequency or rate.

Rule of correspondence. Operational definition; a measurement.

Scholastic philosopher. Philosopher of the church, such as Aquinas or Augustine.

Scientific problem. A problem that can be solved with the methods of science.

Semantics. The study of the relation of signs to objects or words to things.

Sense experience. Whatever occurs when the senses sense.

Solipsism. The view that all one can know is one's own sense experience.

Subjective idealism. The doctrine that "to be is to be perceived" espoused by George Berkeley.

Syllogism. A formal, logical argument in which the acceptance of two premises as true seems to compel the acceptance of a third which follows from them.

Syntactics. The study of the relation of signs to signs or words to words.

System. A comprehensive and consistent, but not necessarily logically formalized, approach to psychology such as those of Guthrie, Tolman, and Skinner.

Teleology.   The study of ends; the belief that the future determines the present.

Topography.   The pattern or organization of something such as a response.

Topology.   The spatial relations between the characteristics of one thing and something else, such as a stimulus and the areas of the brain excited by it.

Variable.   Something that varies, such as the intensity of light or the frequency of response.

Vitalism.   The belief in a vital element or life as a special property of animate objects.

Volition.   Related to will, willing, will power, or choice.

Voluntarist.   One who holds that at least some events are not determined by a prior event, except, perhaps, that of will.

Zoomorphism.   The assignment, by either animals or humans, of animal characteristics to humans.

References

Abelson, R., & Nielsen, K. Ethics, history of. In P. Edwards (Ed.), *The encyclopedia of philosophy* (Vol. 3). New York: Macmillan and Free Press, 1967. Pp. 81-117.

Allport, G. The productive paradoxes of William James. *Psychological Review*, 1943, *50*, 95-120.

Aronson, L.R., et al. *Development and evolution of behavior: Essays in memory of T.C. Schneirla.* San Francisco: W.H. Freeman, 1970.

Bacon, F. *Advancement of learning and novum organum* (Rev. ed.). New York: Colonial Press, 1900.

Barnett, S.A. *Instinct and intelligence: Behavior of animals and man.* Englewood Cliffs: Prentice-Hall, 1967.

Beach, F.A. The descent of instinct. *Psychological Review*, 1955, *62*, 401-10.

References

Berlyne, D.E. *Conflict, arousal, and curiosity.* New York: McGraw-Hill, 1960.

Bindra, D. *Motivation: A systematic reinterpretation.* New York: Ronald Press, 1959.

Bolles, R.C. *Theory of motivation.* New York: Harper and Row, 1967.

Boring, E.G. *A history of experimental psychology* (2nd ed.). New York: Appleton-Century-Crofts, 1957. *(a)*

––––––. When is human behavior predetermined? *Scientific Monthly,* April 1957, pp. 189-96. *(b)*

Capretta, P.J. *A history of psychology in outline: From its origins to the present.* New York: Dell, 1967.

Carnap, R. *Meaning and necessity: A study in semantics and modal logic.* Chicago: University of Chicago Press, 1956.

Corso, J.F. *The experimental psychology of sensory behavior.* New York: Holt, Rinehart, and Winston, 1967.

Darwin, C. *The expression of the emotions in man and animals.* London: Murray, 1873.

––––––. Emotions as serviceable associated habits. In W.S. Sahakian (Ed.), *History of psychology: A source book in systematic psychology.* Itasca, Ill.: Peacock, 1968. Pp. 183-86.

Descartes, R. Meditations on first philosophy. In E.S. Haldane & G.R.T. Ross (Trans.), *The philosophical works of Descartes* (Vol. 1). New York: Cambridge University Press, 1931.

Estes, W.K., et al. *Modern learning theory: A critical analysis of five examples.* New York: Appleton-Century-Crofts, 1954.

Feigl, H. Notes on causality. In H. Feigl & M. Brodbeck (Eds.), *Readings in the philosophy of science.* New York: Appleton-Century-Crofts, 1953.

References

_____. Philosophical embarrassments of psychology. *American Psychologist*, 1959, *14*, 115-28.

_____. The "orthodox" view of theories: Remarks in defense as well as critique. In H. Feigl & G. Maxwell (Eds.), *Minnesota studies in the philosophy of science* (Vol. 4). Minneapolis: University of Minnesota Press, 1970. Pp. 3-16.

Guthrie, E.R. *The psychology of learning* (Rev. ed.). New York: Harper and Brothers, 1952.

Hediger, H. *The psychology and behavior of animals in zoos and circuses*. New York: Dover, 1968.

Heidbreder, E. *Seven psychologies*. New York: Appleton-Century-Crofts, 1933.

Herrnstein, R.J., & Boring, E.G. *A source book in the history of psychology*. Cambridge: Harvard University Press, 1965.

Hinde, R.A. Critique of energy models of motivation. In D. Bindra & J. Stewart (Eds.), *Motivation: Selected readings*. Baltimore: Penguin Books, 1966. Pp. 34-45.

Hull, C.L. *Principles of behavior: An introduction to behavior theory*. New York: Appleton-Century-Crofts, 1943.

_____. *A behavior system*. New Haven: Yale University Press, 1952.

Hume, D. *A treatise of human nature*. L.A. Selby-Bigge (Ed.). London: Oxford University Press, 1888.

_____. *An inquiry concerning human understanding*. C.W. Hendel (Ed.). New York: Liberal Arts Press, 1955.

Immergluck, L. Determinism-freedom in contemporary psychology, an ancient problem revisited. *American Psychologist*, 1964, *19*, 270-81.

James, W. *The principles of psychology* (Vols. 1 & 2). New York: Dover, 1950.

References

Kaplan, A. *The conduct of inquiry: Methodology for behavioral science.* San Francisco: Chandler, 1964.

Katz, J.J. *The problem of induction and its solution.* Chicago: University of Chicago Press, 1962.

Keller, F.S., & Schoenfeld, W.N. *Principles of psychology: A systematic text in the science of behavior.* New York: Appleton-Century-Crofts, 1950.

Kendler, H. "What is learned?"—a theoretical blind alley. In H. Goldstein, et al. (Eds.), *Controversial issues in learning.* New York: Appleton-Century-Crofts, 1965. Pp. 20-30.

Klein, D.B. *A history of scientific psychology: Its origins and philosophical backgrounds.* New York: Basic Books, 1970.

Koch, S. Behavior as "intrinsically" regulated: Work notes towards a pre-theory of phenomena called "motivational." In M.R. Jones (Ed.), *Nebraska symposium on motivation.* Lincoln: University of Nebraska Press, 1956. Pp. 42-87.

————. Epilogue. In S. Koch (Ed.), *Psychology: A study of a science* (Vol. 3). New York: McGraw-Hill, 1959. Pp. 729-88.

————. Psychology and emerging conceptions of knowledge as unitary. In T.W. Wann (Ed.), *Behaviorism and phenomenology: Contrasting bases for modern psychology.* Chicago: University of Chicago Press, 1964. Pp. 1-45.

Kohler, W. *The place of value in a world of facts.* New York: Liverright Publishing Co., 1938.

Lundin, R.W. *Theories and systems of psychology.* Lexington, Mass. D.C. Heath, 1972.

MacCorquodale, K., & Meehl, P.E. Operational validity of intervening constructs. In M.H. Marx (Ed.), *Psychological theory.* New York: Macmillan, 1951. Pp. 103-11.

References

Madsen, K.B. *Theories of motivation: A comparative study of modern theories of motivation* (4th ed.). Kent, Ohio: Kent State University Press, 1968.

Margenau, H. *The nature of physical reality: A philosophy of modern physics.* New York: McGraw-Hill, 1950.

Marx, M.H. The general nature of theory construction. In M.H. Marx (Ed.), *Psychological theory: Contemporary readings.* New York: Macmillan, 1951. Pp. 4-19.

_____ . The general nature of theory construction. In M.H. Marx (Ed.), *Theories in contemporary psychology.* New York: Macmillan, 1963. Pp. 4-46.

_____ . Theory construction and evaluation. In M.H. Marx (Ed.), *Learning: Theories.* New York: Macmillan, 1970. Pp. 3-45.

Marx, M.H., & Hillix, W.W. *Systems and theories in psychology.* New York: McGraw-Hill, 1963.

McDougall, W. *Body and mind: A history and a defense of animism.* New York: Macmillan, 1928.

McGuigan, F.J. *Experimental psychology: A methodological approach* (2nd ed.). Englewood Cliffs, N.J.: Prentice-Hall, 1968.

Mill, J.S. *A system of logic: Ratiocinative and inductive.* London: Longmans, Green and Co., 1936.

Moore, G.E. *Principia ethica.* Cambridge: Cambridge University Press, 1959.

Morgan, C.L. On Lloyd Morgan's canon. In R.J. Herrnstein & E.G. Boring (Eds.), *A source book in the history of psychology.* Cambridge: Harvard University Press, 1966. Pp. 462-68.

Muenzinger, K.F. *Psychology: The science of behavior.* New York: Harper, 1942.

Pavlov, I.P. Scientific study of the so-called psychical processes in the higher animals. In W. Dennis

References

(Ed.), *Readings in the history of psychology*. Cambridge: Harvard University Press, 1966. Pp. 455-61.

Peters, H.N. Affect and emotion. In M.H. Marx (Ed.), *Theories in contemporary psychology*. New York: Macmillan, 1963.

Peters, R.S. *Brett's history of psychology*. Cambridge: MIT Press, 1965.

Pickard-Cambridge, W.A. Topica and de sophisticis elenchis. In W.D. Ross (Ed.), *The works of Aristotle*. Oxford: Clarendon Press, 1928.

Reichenbach, H. *The rise of scientific philosophy*. Berkeley: University of California Press, 1951.

Rogers, C.R., & Skinner, B.F. Some issues concerning the control of human behavior. *Science*, 1965, *124*, 1057-66.

Romanes, G.J. On comparative psychology. In R.J. Herrnstein & E.G. Boring (Eds.), *A source book in the history of psychology*. Cambridge: Harvard University Press, 1965.

Russell, B. *The problems of philosophy*. London: Holt and Co., 1912.

———. On the notion of cause, with application to the free-will problem. In H. Feigl & M. Brodbeck (Eds.), *Readings in the philosophy of science*. New York: Appleton-Century-Crofts, 1953.

Russell, W.A. *Milestones in motivation: Contributions to the psychology of drive and purpose*. New York: Appleton-Century-Crofts, 1970.

Ryle, G. *The concept of mind*. New York: Barnes & Noble, 1949.

Skinner, B.F. *The behavior of organisms: An experimental analysis*. New York: Appleton-Century-Crofts, 1938.

References

_____. Are theories of learning necessary? *Psychological Review*, 1950, 57, 193-216.

_____. *Science and human behavior*. New York: Free Press, 1953.

_____. *Cumulative record* (Enlarged ed.). New York: Appleton-Century-Crofts, 1961.

_____. *The technology of teaching*. New York: Appleton-Century-Crofts, 1968.

_____. *Contingencies of reinforcement: A theoretical analysis*. New York: Appleton-Century-Crofts, 1969.

_____. *Beyond freedom and dignity*. New York: Knopf, 1971.

Spence, K.W. The nature of theory construction in contemporary psychology. *Psychological Review*, 1944, *51*, 47-68.

_____. *Behavior theory and conditioning*. New Haven: Yale University Press, 1956.

_____. The emphasis on basic functions. In M.H. Marx (Ed.), *Theories in contemporary psychology*. New York: Macmillan, 1963. Pp. 272-86.

Staats, A.W., & Staats, C.K. *Complex human behavior: A systematic extension of learning principles*. New York: Holt, Rinehart, and Winston, 1963.

Stevens, S.S. Mathematics, measurement, and psychophysics. In S.S. Stevens (Ed.), *Handbook of experimental psychology*. New York: Wiley, 1951. Pp. 1-49.

Thorndike, E.L. Science and values. *Science*, 1936, *83*, 1-8.

Tolman, E.C. Prediction of vicarious trial and error by means of the schematic sowbug. *Psychological Review*, 1939, *46*, 318-36.

_____. *Purposive behavior in animals and men*. New

References

York: Appleton-Century-Crofts, 1967.

Turner, M.B. *Philosophy and the science of behavior.* New York: Appleton-Century-Crofts, 1967.

―――. *Psychology and the philosophy of science.* New York: Appleton-Century-Crofts, 1968.

―――. *Realism and the explanation of behavior.* New York: Appleton-Century-Crofts, 1971.

Wann, T.W. *Behaviorism and phenomenology: Contrasting bases for modern psychology.* Chicago: University of Chicago Press, 1964.

Waters, R.H. Mechanomorphism: A new term for an old mode of thought. *Psychological Review,* 1948, *55,* 139-42.

Watson, J.B. Psychology as the behaviorist views it. *Psychological Review,* 1913, *20,* 158-77.

Watson, R.I. *The great psychologists* (3rd ed.). Philadelphia: Lippincott, 1971.

Wertheimer, M. *Fundamental issues in psychology.* New York: Holt, Rinehart, and Winston, 1972.

Wolman, B.B. Does psychology need its own philosophy of science? *American Psychologist,* 1971, *26,* 877-86.

Index

Index

Cause: as functional, 55-56

"Cause and effect": special meaning, 51

Chance: and freedom, 120, 121

Common sense: and purpose, 172; solutions, 164

Constant conjunction: in causation, 58-59, 143

Construction: in explanation, 51-52; metaphysics and reification, 100

Contiguity: in causation, 57-59, 63, 143

Control: and S-R law, 85

Convention: discussed, 175-76; and distinction between facts and values, 161, 175; and philosophical problems, 91

Correlation: in causation, 60, 63; and laws, 84

Correlational relationships: as laws, 91

Data: defined, 80

Debate: Rogers and Skinner, 125-28

Deduction: in explanation, 47-49, 52; and rationalism, 133-34; and theory, 73; and traditional rationalism, 47

Deductive meta-theory: discussed, 74-75

Dependent variable: defined, 84; as "effect," 50, 61, 62; in explanation, 51

Description: as pseudoexplanation, 37

Determinism: as an assumption, 127; and freedom, 119-21; as presupposition of science, 124-25; and voluntarism, 120

Double aspect hypothesis: discussed, 17

Dualisms: listed, 15

Effect: law of, 107-8

Emergentism: defined, 106

Empiricism: and anthropomorphism, 101; defined, 133; in explanation, 49-51; and mind, 165-66; and phenomenalism, 31

About the Author

Dr. Eacker is associate professor of psychology at Whitman College. His research interests include the history and philosophy of psychology, especially as it is considered a science of behavior. He has published on these subjects in the *American Psychologist* and the *Catalog of Selected Documents in Psychology*.